Collins

need to know?

Cognitive
Behavioural
Therapy

Carolyn Boyes

Collins

First published in 2008 by Collins
an imprint of
HarperCollins Publishers
77–85 Fulham Palace Road
London W6 8JB

www.collins.co.uk

A catalogue record for this book is available from
the British Library

Text: Carolyn Boyes
Editor: Grapevine Publishing Services Ltd
Series design: Mark Thomson
Front cover photograph: iStockPhoto
Back cover photographs: iStockPhoto

ISBN 978-0-00-727034-7

Printed and bound by Printing Express Ltd,
Hong Kong

Contents

Introduction 6

1 The basics of CBT 8

2 Identifying faulty thinking 24

3 The foundation of change 58

4 Setting goals 76

5 Changing thoughts and feelings 86

6 Overcoming resistance to change 102

7 Anger 112

8 Anxiety 132

9 Depression 148

10 Stress and tension 166

11 Self-esteem 180

Useful organizations 190

Further reading 191

Free online CBT resources 191

Index 192

Introduction

Cognitive Behavioural Therapy (CBT) is becoming more and more popular as a highly respected and scientifically tested treatment for a range of psychological problems. It is a systematic therapy that helps you to feel a greater sense of well-being and to overcome problem emotions.

We all have ups and downs. Some of us experience strong or persistent unpleasant feelings we would like to get rid of. If you are in this position this book will help you to find routes you can take to overcome these emotions and practical methods you can use straight away.

If you don't have any particular problems currently but are just intrigued to find out more about the theory and practice of CBT, you will find that here.

Finally, if you are considering consulting a professional such as a doctor or CBT therapist about a problem, you may find it useful to read the book first or alongside your consultation.

About *Need to know? Cognitive Behavioural Therapy*
Because this is not a book written for specialists, it does not go into detail about every type of problem for which CBT can be used, but the principles outlined here for specific problem areas in the book can be extended and applied to problems that may not be covered.

1. The first part of the book covers all the theory:
• Chapter 1 includes the history of how and why CBT evolved, to the basic underlying theory and how CBT differs from other forms of therapy.
• Chapter 2 looks at how the way you think can cause unpleasant emotions.

• Chapter 3 is concerned with the nature of change and the beliefs that help you to create the change you want.

2. The second part of the book (Chapters 4 and 5) focuses on taking action. With CBT you do not have to look into your past to find the root of current problems and move forward. Instead, you can concentrate on how your current thinking affects your current feelings.

Need to know? CBT will show you how to overcome any blocks and resistance to change. You will learn to develop goals for the life you want and to identify unwanted thoughts and feelings. Finally, you will acquire new strategies for bringing more pleasant emotions into your life.

3. The third part of the book highlights issues behind particular emotional disorders and lays out specific tips for dealing with them.

4. The Appendix includes contacts for organizations and other resources should you want to know more about CBT or if you want to find a therapist to work with.

Using *Need to know? CBT*

If you are using this book as a self-help tool, you may find it helpful to refer back to the theory of CBT as you go through the worksheets. Taking your time reading through the book will help you to think about where you are now, your current beliefs and feelings and your goals for a new life with healthy thoughts and feelings.

1 The basics of CBT

Cognitive Behavioural Therapy (CBT) is used to treat emotional and behavioural problems, from depression to anxiety or addictions. In this chapter you will learn about the basic principles of CBT – what it is and why it could be effective as a therapeutic tool for you.

The basics of CBT

Cognitive behavioural therapy (CBT) is a type of psychotherapy that combines behaviour modification and cognitive therapy. It focuses on cognition (belief), emotion (feeling) and behaviour (action).

must know

The meaning of Cognitive Behavioural Therapy
• The 'cognitive' in cognitive behavioural therapy refers to our thoughts and beliefs.
• The 'behavioural' refers to behavioural modification. Behavioural therapy focuses on the relationship between our problems, our behaviour and our thoughts.
• The 'therapy' describes the structured approach used with a sufferer to overcome a disorder.

Why use CBT?

CBT highlights how your irrational thoughts (beliefs and assumptions) determine your feelings and affect your choices of your actions and behaviour. The focus of the therapy is to eliminate disorders such as depression, anxiety or phobias. It aims to change your thinking and feeling patterns to allow in more helpful thoughts, which in turn will produce more helpful feelings and new behaviours.

CBT is a rational process comprising a set of useful psychological and emotional tools which are available whenever needed. You can then look at your goals, the kind of life you want and where you are now in relation to this ideal.

As a therapy, CBT demystifies a person's actions and reactions to uncover reasons why they might experience negative thoughts, anxiety, depression or fear, then to challenge and eventually change them.

Several studies of psychotherapeutic methods point to CBT as one of the most effective therapies for treating depression and anxiety. In fact, research shows that CBT appears to be more successful than antidepressive medication in treating certain types of depression.

In 2003, NICE – the UK Government body advising on how best to treat different illnesses and disorders

– recommended that CBT be used as either the first-line or an additional treatment for anxiety, depression, eating disorders, obsessive compulsive disorder, post-traumatic stress disorder and schizophrenia.

What's more, you can learn to use CBT yourself without a therapist present to combat unwanted automatic thoughts, feelings and behaviour.

The history of CBT

The foundations of CBT go back to the early part of the 20th century. Based on the work of Pavlov and other Russian researchers, it was discovered that emotional responses such as anxiety or fear can be conditioned. In Pavlov's famous experiments dogs were given food when a bell was rung. After a number of repetitions, the dogs started to salivate in response to the bell – they had been conditioned to respond to an external stimulus.

This is known as 'classical conditioning' and the Russian researchers used it as the basis for further research. They found out that if animals were given an electric shock at the same time as being shown a red light, they would eventually respond to the red light alone with fear and an increase in heart rate. The red light would have become a 'conditioned fear stimulus'.

Conditioning and behaviour

Later another principle of conditioning known as 'the law of effect' was developed. Three researchers in the USA – Thorndike, Tolman and Guthrie – discovered that if a particular behaviour was consistently rewarded it was likely to reoccur.

must know

What can CBT treat?
CBT can be used to treat a wide range of disorders and unwanted feelings. These include:

• Stress and tension
• Depression
• Anxiety
• Anger
• Sleeping problems
• Guilt
• Chronic fatigue syndrome
• Mood swings
• Facial tics
• Childhood problems
• Relationship break-up
• Phobias including agoraphobia and social phobia
• Schizophrenia
• Panic disorders
• Post-traumatic stress
• Obsessive compulsive disorder
• Bulimia
• Chronic non-malignant pain.

must know

Self-talk
Automatic thoughts or
self-talk are thoughts
laden with negative
emotions and are
often unconscious.

This principle was then extended to show that *any* behaviour could be reinforced: 'positive reinforcement' happens when a behaviour occurs frequently, or more strongly, because it is reinforced by positive consequences; for example, praise or another reward. 'Negative reinforcement' happens when behaviour happens frequently because it is followed by *the lack of* anticipated negative consequences – for example, not being told off. These principles were fundamental to behavioural therapy, which became accepted in the second half of the 20th century as a useful therapy for disorders such as phobias and obsessions.

The 1960s and Aaron Beck
The breakthrough for CBT came in the 1960s. Aaron Beck, an American psychiatrist and psychotherapist, observed that there was a link between the self-talk of his patients and their feelings. He described the negative internal dialogue running in his patients' minds as 'automatic thoughts', a term used interchangeably with 'hot thoughts', to describe thoughts laden with negative emotions.

He discovered that his patients were not always aware of these hot thoughts or of their effect on their feelings. However, if a patient learned to identify these emotion-linked thoughts they could learn to overcome their problems.

Cognitive Therapy
Beck's methods became known as cognitive therapy – 'cognitive' referring to the important role played by thoughts and beliefs in producing unpleasant feelings. It has since evolved into cognitive

behavioural therapy as it has become recognized that behavioural techniques can also help the therapeutic process.

Another important influence on modern CBT is Dr Albert Ellis (see page 14).

How CBT works

Beck's theory at the heart of CBT is that:

It is not a particular situation or event that directly causes us problem feelings but the meaning we attach to this situation – our 'self-talk'.

This self-talk or meaning we attribute to events originates in childhood experiences. Over time we set up rigid thinking patterns which trigger automatic reactions to situations. These patterns are unconscious and because they become rigid may be resistant to change without deliberate and effective analysis and challenge. The meaning we attach to events can also be called a 'core belief' or 'rules for living'.

Our thoughts and beliefs may work well for us in some situations, while in others they may cause us negative reactions. As rational emotive therapist Dr Maxie Mautsby put it: 'Words are to humans as the bell was to Pavlov's dog.' What we say to ourselves, 'our self-talk', is all important.

Basic premise of CBT
Our thoughts produce our feelings.
The model of how this works is sometimes referred to as the 'hot cross bun' model. It assumes that when we have a negative reaction to a situation it is because the meaning we have attached to it causes an automatic conditioned response.

must know

Problem feelings
Our problem feelings are not caused directly by a situation or event, but instead by the meaning that we attach to this situation – our self-talk.

watch out

Meaning is subjective
There is no such thing as a negative or positive situation or event. Your reactions are caused by the meanings you have unconsciously or consciously attached to the event.

What you think about a situation triggers certain feelings (including unwanted physical sensations).
Your feelings lead to actions, i.e. your behaviour (wanted or unwanted).

Types of problems

According to Dr Albert Ellis, who developed Rational Emotive Therapy (a form of CBT), there are two main types of problem.

1. **Practical problems** are obstacles we encounter that prevent us from reaching goals. For example, a cancelled cheque may mean you have no money in your bank account to pay an important bill.

2. **Emotional problems** are our reactions to a perceived problem, i.e. the upset you feel about the cheque being cancelled. The practical problem is real – it exists no matter how you react to it. The emotional problem in contrast is your unconscious choice about what meaning and reaction to give to the practical problem.

In addition, there is sometimes a third type of problem:

3. **Imagined problems** are the idea that a practical problem exists when it does not. Perhaps the cheque has not in fact been cancelled or the situation can be rectified in a few minutes.

When a problem occurs, you choose how to react to it. When you react negatively, it is generally for two reasons:

1. You have got the facts wrong – the situation is not as you see it.

2. You have got the facts right and believe that the situation inevitably has to lead to a particular negative emotional response. Your thinking may be entirely conditioned – i.e. you may not be aware of the thoughts leading you to produce these emotions, only that you must respond to the situation and the response appears to be unavoidable.

Thinking

You may wonder: 'If my thoughts aren't useful to me why did I learn them to begin with?' Or: 'Why do I have different reactions from other people in similar situations?'

The first way you learn to think is through observing how other people do it. When you are a child, you acquire thoughts, beliefs and deeply held values or observations about the world through your parents and peers.

Secondly, you acquire thoughts through conditioning: positive and negative reinforcement may influence our responses to situations (see page 12). If you are consistently rewarded or punished for thinking in a particular way you become more or less likely to think that way in the future.

How we produce good or bad thoughts and feelings

To diagnose how we have produced negative feelings and behaviour (and to get rid of them), CBT uses a tool known as the ABC model (see overleaf) to break a problem down into its component parts.

must know

Negative thinking
A pattern of negative thinking produces a problem cycle of emotions. The way to break the cycle is to recognize that the negative thoughts are not inevitable, correct or natural at all. With practice a patient can learn to recognize negative thought patterns and set up new habits to correct any thinking bias.

The ABC model

A The activating event (or what you are 'AWARE of'): the situation, event or problem you are facing acts as a trigger to set off a pattern of feelings and behaviours. This may be an external event in the present, or a future event you are anticipating. It may also be an internal event: a picture in your mind or a memory.

B Beliefs: your automatic (negative/toxic) beliefs and thoughts, which include your unconscious rules, values and principles for yourself, other people and the world. The self-talk determines the meaning you attach to the activating event.

C Consequences: these include your emotions and physical feelings and your actions and behaviour (wanted or unwanted).

Each of these areas affects the others to set up an automatic and sometimes ongoing vicious circle that makes you feel bad and even may create new negative situations.

Imagine that you encounter a situation to which you have attached a particular meaning. You may perceive this situation as difficult or negative. What happens is that the encounter triggers a series of negative thoughts and then negative feelings. This sequence may then lead into a self-feeding circle of automatic thoughts, feelings and behaviour. When this cycle begins it can build up in intensity, generating more and more negative self-talk and unhelpful beliefs.

Often you may be aware of the type of situation that creates negative emotions but not of the thoughts triggered in between. In other words, what seems to be happening is:

A (activating event/ aware of) ➜ ***C (consequences = emotional reaction)***
You are not aware of the fact that there is a B in the middle of the pattern.

A (activating event/ aware of) ➜ ***B (belief) about the situation*** ➜ ***C (consequences = emotional reaction)***
What you think about the trigger to your emotion is so habitual and well conditioned that it has become totally outside your conscious awareness. These hidden thoughts are known as automatic or reflex thoughts.

Automatic negative thoughts
Automatic thoughts can be very useful. For example, when you are driving, it is a useful reaction to slam your foot on the brake if a car pulls out in front of you. However, it may not be a useful reaction to get angry if your neighbour frowns in your direction – it may be because of a conditioned automatic thought from a childhood situation that has come to mean 'a frown means a person is going to hurt me'. The thought may have once protected you, but now it is out of context and irrational in your current situation.

The next chapter looks in detail at different thinking mistakes that can lead to a negative ABC pattern.

First, though, here are some general principles about how thoughts and beliefs take hold and how you can challenge them if they are producing unwanted feelings.

Thoughts – basic principles
A thought can be:
• An internal memory of a past event
• An internal image of a future situation
• Your rules about how you 'should' appear and behave in a situation, how you are allowed to behave

must know

Quick thinking
An automatic or reflex thought is a thought that has been so well conditioned that it is triggered in as little as a ten thousandth of a second. Because it happens so quickly, you may not be aware that you thought anything at all. You just have the impression that a feeling was triggered without any thought happening in between.

• Your rules about how other people 'should' appear and behave towards you
• Your anticipation of future behaviour from yourself and others
• Your view of the consequences of this behaviour.

Your thoughts can be a mixture of helpful and unhelpful. Some thoughts are a useful reaction to the situation and are essentially rational. Others are 'thinking errors' or 'faulty thinking': they are irrational and feed negative emotions and irrational behaviour.

Beliefs
Our thoughts spring from our beliefs. The beliefs you hold determine the meaning you give to an external or internal event. A belief about yourself or others can trigger an onslaught of automatic thoughts in your mind when you encounter a particular situation.

Negative thoughts are habitual. You don't sit down and consciously think them. They come into your mind automatically. Although these thoughts are only based on biased 'beliefs' because they come into our minds so automatically, you may think of them as facts.

Beliefs tend to:
• be about you and how you view your identity, e.g. 'I am a lazy person'.
• be about other people, e.g. 'He/she doesn't like me'.
• stop you from taking action, e.g. 'I can't show my emotions'.
• make you take action, e.g. 'I need to be nice to people or they won't like me'.

It is important to recognize that a belief and a fact are very different. A belief is simply an opinion that you hold about yourself, other people or the world and its events. It may be supported by evidence that you have gathered, but that doesn't make it true.

Feelings – basic principles

Here are some basic principles about feelings to bear in mind (taken from Albert Ellis's Model of Rational Emotive Therapy).

• It is important to distinguish between unproductive and productive feelings: productive feelings lead to effective behaviour.

• Unproductive feelings (also labelled negative, 'uncomfortable' or 'toxic') lead to ineffective behaviour.

• Some physiological feelings are unconscious. You can't use willpower to stop them. For example, pain in the gut or heart palpitations.

• Some emotional feelings (like anxiety and jealousy) which are triggered by external situations are learned and can be controlled.

Learning to produce positive feelings and behaviour

By understanding your ABC cycles you can interrupt unhelpful patterns and challenge your thinking to produce new, more helpful and rational thoughts which will alter your feelings – even down to the physical reactions in your body.

Of course the same automatic pattern also applies in situations to which you have attached a positive meaning, leading to a cycle of positive reactions.

must know

The 'B' in ABC
To change your irrrational beliefs, first identify them. If you are only aware of the A and the C in your ABCs, ask yourself 'in order to have this reaction to this situation, what would I have to believe?'

Breaking the negative ABC cycle

Changing your thoughts will change your feelings which will, in turn, lead to different behaviour.

If you have uncomfortable physical or emotional feelings about a situation, challenge your thoughts. By learning to identify faulty thinking patterns you will learn to get rid of 'toxic' emotions and live in a happier and healthier way.

Activating Situation
Events
People
Future

Beliefs
Pictures of the present and future
Memories
Self-talk, automatic thoughts

Consequences: emotions
Pleasant reactions
Unpleasant reactions
Feelings in the body

Consequences: behaviours
Constructive
Destructive

Symptom stress

It is not only a particular situation that causes negative emotions. Some people will feel emotional distress about the fact that they feel bad rather than about the situation that triggered the original feeling. This has been called 'symptom stress' by Dr Albert Ellis. For example, a person may feel:
• afraid of feeling anxious
• depressed about being depressed
• anxious about being afraid
• depressed about having a problem
• afraid that they will always have their problem

Example of a **negative** ABC pattern:

Activating event/what you are aware of: your boyfriend tells you he wants to end his relationship with you because he has found someone else.

Beliefs: the meaning you give the situation and automatic thoughts: this proves that I am unlovable and other people are better than me.

Consequences: emotional reaction – a feeling of upset and depression.

Physical reaction: you feel sick and cry.

An alternative **positive** ABC pattern

Activating event/what you are aware of: your boyfriend tells you he wants to end his relationship with you because he has found someone else.

Beliefs: the meaning you give the situation and automatic thoughts: 'My boyfriend does not appreciate me. We are very different. This is just proof of incompatibility. It is good that we are both moving on – this will free me up to meet someone with whom I can have a better relationship.'

Consequences: emotional reaction – calmness with some sense of loss or relief.

• depressed, feeling that they are the only person who has this type of problem.

These feelings can be very destructive for a sufferer as they are often left with the idea that they can't bear the emotions they are experiencing, which may lead directly to unhelpful behaviour in an attempt to relieve the stress of the situation – for example, drinking, overeating or taking drugs. Obviously, feeling upset about having a negative emotion serves no useful purpose so is one of the issues that CBT would address.

Next steps?

You can practise CBT through this book or through an on-line programme. The book lays out the basics of CBT and provides sheets to challenge your own thinking that you can photocopy and fill in at any time without a therapist present.

CBT can be carried out individually or with a group. It tends to be a short-term therapy compared with many other psychotherapies. Therapists may suggest only a few months or even six or eight sessions for some problems. Unlike some psychotherapies or talking therapies, CBT concentrates on what your thoughts are now about your current situation. It does not require extensive analysis of your childhood or what has happened in the past.

In this, CBT has some similarities to Neuro-Linguistic Programming (NLP) which also breaks down the automatic strategies our brains use and teaches ways to modify them to produce new behaviours and emotions to help us overcome our difficulties.

Many therapists use an assessment in an initial session to recognize and screen for feelings such as depression and anxiety.

Session structure

A session may last up to one hour during which the client discusses the problem with the therapist and looks at new strategies and ways of thinking to combat an issue. Sometimes, sessions will be spaced out two or three weeks apart.

Between sessions the patient is expected to implement what they have learned and to identify thoughts and feelings. Sometimes they may be given material or books to read.

In some cases you may expect improvement even after just half of your sessions. For some conditions, you may be given drug treatment at the same time as therapy.

Whichever route you take remember that being persistent is important. You will learn how to solve your problems and how to change your distorted thinking only by taking action and aiming towards clear goals. You need to be prepared to put the work in to get the results.

Even with a therapist, you as the patient are an active participant and not a passive observer or listener, so you can expect to learn new skills.

want to know more?
• CBT may be available on the NHS. If so, the therapist will often be a clinical psychologist or psychiatrist.
• For general information contact the Association for Behavioural and Cognitive Therapies www.abct.org or The International Association for Cognitive Psychotherapy www.cognitivetherapy association.org
• Chapter 5 has more information on ABC sheets.
• Read Chapter 6 for advice on overcoming blocks.

2 Identifying faulty thinking

The emotions you feel come about because of your thoughts. Unfortunately, the brain cannot distinguish between rational and irrational thoughts. One of the goals of CBT is to identify the types of thinking that cause you problem emotions.

Identifying faulty thinking

Every time you think about a situation it produces a reaction inside you (a feeling) and an outcome in the real world that may be or may not be the one you would most desire. Some of your thoughts are not helpful to you. They produce an interpretation of the world that feeds negative beliefs, emotions and behaviours.

must know

Thinking errors
Faulty thinking causes us to interpret memories and thoughts about the future in a negative way, resulting in unpleasant emotions.

Your thinking

Some thoughts we can label as 'faulty thinking', 'warpy' thinking or as 'thinking errors'. These thoughts distort our thinking in a way that causes us to expect the worst and to feel unpleasant emotions.

Your thinking consists of memories of the past, the pictures you have inside your head of the current situation and the pictures you have of possible futures resulting from this current situation.

Added to this is a whole host of other thoughts, including how you appear to yourself and others involved in the situation, your predictions of your own and other people's behaviours, and your anticipations of the likely consequences of these behaviours.

CBT highlights ten main types of faulty thinking (see 'must know' boxes starting on page 27). By understanding which types of faulty thinking you habitually use, you can challenge and replace them with more useful ways of thinking to produce a healthier response to events and situations.

All-or-nothing thinking

All or nothing thinking means viewing things in black and white terms or, in other words, as everything or nothing. This way of thinking excludes the possibility that there is a middle ground. But of course in real life there is often a halfway house of things happening in degrees.

Language clues

Listen to the language you use to detect your own all-or-nothing thinking. Watch out for the words 'am' and 'is'. They may be being used to identify someone as completely one thing or another. Any words that imply *perfectionism* are an example of this type of thinking.

• *Our relationship is totally spoilt now.*
• *She is fat.*
• *I am not perfect.*
• *It's a complete waste of time trying to give up smoking.*
• *Men are all untrustworthy.*
• *There's no point me saving money. I am rubbish at saving.*

Problems with 'all-or-nothing' thinking

• All-or-nothing thinking interferes with goals. If you set a goal and have a setback on the way to it, then you are likely to give up on that goal if you are thinking in an all-or-nothing way.
• You may interpret a single piece of evidence, an event or occurrence as an ongoing pattern of defeat.
• Perfectionism invites failure. Very few things in real life are able to achieve 100 per cent. There is often a shortfall, even a very small one. If you tend to be

perfectionist in your thinking you are likely to interpret the most minuscule shortfall as a failure.

Examples of all-or-nothing thinking

• *You want to lose weight. You set a goal to lose 10 pounds. You start by sticking to a calorie-controlled diet, then three days into the diet you are invited to a party where you indulge in two slices of birthday cake. If you are an all-or-nothing thinker you might think, 'My diet is completely ruined now so I might as well give up!' If you accept a middle way of thinking, you might think 'It was just two slices of birthday cake. I will carry on with my calorie-controlled diet tomorrow'.*

• *You want to learn French. You set a goal to learn to read a newspaper in French within a year by going to French classes. However, you find that you are slipping behind your classmates. Instead of measuring your progress against the goal and adjusting the goal or spending more time studying, you simply decide, 'I am bad at languages' and give up.*

How to challenge all-or-nothing thinking

1. **Allow for a middle ground in your thinking**. It is helpful to consider thinking in terms of degrees of a scale. For example, where do you sit on a scale where totally underweight is at one end and totally overweight is at the other end? Or, if your boyfriend lets you down, where on a scale of trustworthiness does he now sit?

2. **Accept the idea of failure as feedback rather than as an end to whatever action you are taking towards your goals**. Feedback just reminds you to be realistic. You've made a mistake. So what. It's just a reminder that you are human. Now carry on taking action towards what you want. If you have to adjust the type of action you need to take that's fine.

3. **Instead of either/or, how about both/and?** You can be both able to learn French and be not as good as your classmates.

You can be able to diet and occasionally lapse in your control of calories. Both/and thinking gives you much more leeway to be flexible and experiment with change.

4. As well as 'can't' use 'yet'. So you can't do something, but that doesn't have to be the final answer. If you add the word 'yet' to the statement you will open up the possibility of change. For example, instead of 'I can't speak French' what about 'I can't speak French yet'?

5. Stop being a perfectionist. Recognize the '80/20 rule'. If you are achieving 80 per cent of what you set out to do, you have done very well and can congratulate yourself on a job well done. Eighty per cent means that you have high standards. We are fallible human beings operating in the real world. It is very unlikely you will ever reach 100 per cent.

Overgeneralization

Overgeneralization is a way of exaggerating in thinking. Instead of being very specific in your thinking about a situation, you exaggerate an aspect of it.

Language clues

- *Always*
- *Never*
- *Everybody*
- *Nobody*
- *The world*
- *All*
- *None*

Listen to your language

Sometimes words such as 'always' or 'never' may be accurately used to describe a situation. For example, the statement, 'He never brings me flowers' might be a true description of your experience. But what if the man in question has twice brought you flowers and you use the same sentence to describe the event? What you have done unconsciously is to delete the positive experiences of the past from your mind and overgeneralize the negatives to produce a thinking error.

Examples of overgeneralization
• *I NEVER meet people I like at parties.*
• *I ALWAYS draw the short straw and have to buy a round of drinks.*
• *I ALWAYS get sacked eventually.*
• *My friends ALWAYS end up rejecting me.*
• *I will ALWAYS be lonely.*
• *EVERYONE is better than me at everything.*
• *ALL people who live in towns take drugs.* • *She NEVER hears what I am saying.*

Problems with overgeneralization
• It suggest that a situation is inflexible or final. In other words, it disempowers you by implying that you don't have the ability to change anything.
• Overgeneralization also causes prejudice. For example, 'all Africans are poor', or 'all young people are badly behaved'. If you have leaped to a general conclusion because of one piece of evidence it will cause you to hold opinions that then may become difficult to shift.

How to challenge overgeneralization
1. Be specific in your descriptions. Distinguish between when you use words such as 'always' or 'never' accurately to describe the facts of a situation and when you are generalizing.

2. Be open-minded. Be aware when you are expressing an opinion that may have been formed based on very little evidence. View things on a case by case basis.

3. Question the words that indicate overgeneralization in what you are saying: e.g. Never? Has there ever been a time when she heard you? Everyone? Always? Can you think of any contrary examples?

Keep perspective by looking for evidence that challenges any negative presuppositions you are carrying about yourself and others.

Mental filtering

Mental filtering is the means by which we unconsciously filter information from the world in a way that makes it 'fit in' with our pre-existing opinions and beliefs. If a piece of information comes our way that appears to contradict a deeply held belief about the world, we distort it or delete it in some way to make it fit.

Examples of mental filtering

• *You think, 'I am stupid'. You ignore any evidence that counteracts this idea even though there are many examples, if you look, of things you have learnt to do to a high standard.*

• *You think, 'My life is all terrible'. Yet if asked to list the negative and positive aspects of your life you may well be able to come up with more positives than negatives.*

• *A separating couple think, 'My partner is a horrible, mean person. They never used to be like this. Why did they change?' They ignore all the good things about the person they once fell in love with.*

Problems with mental filtering

• **Being blinkered.** Being in love is a good example of this. Each member of a couple thinks: 'There is no one like my partner. He/she is the most wonderful person in the world.' After a while they stop filtering to the same extent and notice aspects of their partner that they hadn't been aware of before. It appears as if the person has changed. Of course it is really their perspective that has changed.

• **Disqualifying the positive.** Discounting and ignoring the positive aspects of situations goes alongside mental filtering. What you look for is what you get. If you are focused on the negative you may not notice all the positive things. Discounting the positives helps to maintain negative beliefs.

• **Leaping to conclusions.** Coming to a conclusion too quickly without adequate evidence is not necessarily helpful as once again it may cause prejudices against oneself or others.

How to challenge mental filtering

1. Pay attention to sweeping statements. What negative prejudices do you have about yourself? Have you ever caught yourself thinking 'I am' or 'I am not' followed by a negative word such as 'stupid', 'useless' or 'failure'? What about the way you perceive your life? Or your partner? These are just beliefs caused by mental filtering of specific aspects of the situation so that you pick out and dwell on the negative.

2. Hunt for contradictory evidence. Could you be wrong in your opinions? If you were a lawyer in a court case you wouldn't leap to conclusions, you would look for evidence to support any opinions presented in court. Look at all aspects of the situation ; hunt down evidence that disproves your prejudices and supports other ways of thinking. Notice what you believe currently. Now propose a new belief – you don't have to believe it yet. Simply allow it as a possibility and collect evidence to support it. After doing this, notice what you now believe.

Mind reading

Mind reading occurs when we presume that we can read what another person is thinking and then we act on our assumption. We tend to project onto other people our own ways of thinking. In addition we also project what we most fear.

In mind reading there is no room for doubt, i.e. instead of thinking that the other person *may* think in a particular way, we think and act with certainty – 'He/she *definitely* thinks this.'

Examples of mind reading

• *A woman goes on a blind date. She has been on several before. It is the man's first date. She talks for the majority of the conversation. He appears distant during the conversation and at the end of the date does not express any desire to meet up in future. She assumes that he is not interested in her because she is too talkative or too boring. In fact, he is interested in her but as it is his first date he is feeling shy and assumes that if she is interested she will follow up with him.*
• *A man is called into a meeting with his boss and several other colleagues. When he begins talking he notices that his boss changes expression, which he interprets as disapproval. In fact, his boss is worrying that his parking meter is about to run out.*
• *A woman bumps into an old school friend. He says that he will call next week so that they can meet up for a coffee but it never happens. The next time the woman sees him on the street she walks on by. She assumes that she must have said something to offend him. In fact, he had got caught up in a family crisis and had forgotten.*

Problems with mind reading

• **You can't read another person's mind**. It's as simple as that. Each person has their own unique life experiences, ways of thinking, beliefs, attitudes and prejudices. Even when you have known someone for a long time, you may be able to predict *some* of the time how they will respond to a certain situation but not *all* of the time.

• **Jumping to conclusions.** When you mind read and act on the supposed information you have, you may not communicate with the other person as much as if you had not jumped to conclusions. When you guess rather than look for evidence for a particular way of thinking you may well take actions that lead to a negative outcome and reinforce your prejudices.

• **Reading minds is a waste of time.** It is more useful to respond to how someone *acts* rather than what they *might* be *thinking*.

must know

Ten main types of faulty thinking:
4. Mind reading – acting on your assumptions about what other people are thinking.

How to challenge mind reading

1. Challenge your negative assumptions. Recognize that your negative prejudices, insecurities and fears about yourself, other people and the world may be causing you to mind read. Are you drawing a straight line between something you observe and a negative consequence for you as a result of the negative beliefs you hold? If so, carry on gathering information. You may disprove your beliefs. State only the facts of the situation to yourself clearly and wait to draw a conclusion.

2. Communicate, rather than leap to a conclusion. If you do not like the way someone is behaving towards you, instead of assuming that you know the reasons why, talk to them. Discuss with them whether they are willing to talk to you about what they are doing. Are either of you interested in changing your behaviour? Why have the two of you set up this situation?

3. Think of possible alternative reasons. There is an infinite number of reasons for different behaviours. How many other explanations can you find?

Fortune telling

Fortune telling occurs when you leap to a conclusion about what is going to happen in the future and act according to these predictions. When you feel very nervous about an event in advance you may be indulging in negative fortune telling.

It is true that if we know a person or situation very well, we may be able to predict some of their behaviour, but just as with mind reading, this is only a possible or, at the most, probable outcome. We only ever 'might know' the outcome.

Examples of fortune telling

• *You really want your male colleague at the water cooler to ask you out. However, on the basis of past experiences you predict that he is either married or wouldn't be interested, so you ignore him.*

• *You are asked to a ball. You predict that it will be full of people with lots of money who won't be interested in you because you aren't smart enough. You go but your predictions make you so nervous that you hide in a corner most of the time.*

• *You are asked to go on a skiing trip. You have never tried skiing before and predict that you will be bad at it. As a result you refuse the invitation then bemoan the fact that you never have anything fun to do.*

Problems with fortune telling

• **Predicting the future can lead to a self-fulfilling prophecy.** For example, if you are convinced a girlfriend is about to end your relationship, you may start to behave differently towards her, which in turn may lead her to become unhappy with the relationship and end it. If you think you will fail

must know

Ten main types of faulty thinking:
5. Fortune telling – you leap to conclusions by thinking you know what is going to happen.

your maths test you may not take the time to study sufficiently. If you were to ignore your negative predictions and study you might have a very positive outcome.

• **Negative fortune telling stops you taking action**. If you think you know what will happen, why take a risk to move out of your comfort zone, try something new and experiment? Why ever talk to new types of people, try a new sport, go to a new place or learn a new subject? Fortune telling can take the excitement out of life.

How to challenge fortune telling

1. Avoid leaping to conclusions. You don't own a crystal ball. Recognize that your predictions 'might' be true but that isn't the same as being 'definitely true', which in turn means that they might be entirely wrong.

2. Your future can be different from your past. The past is not a straight-line indicator to the future. Just because something happened in the past it doesn't mean that it will necessarily happen in the same way in the future. Just because you went to one dinner party that turned out to be very boring it doesn't mean that the next one will be.

3. Take account of all the evidence. One way to gather evidence, information and facts is to test your predictions. For example, you think that you will fail your examination. What will happen if you study harder than normal?

4. Go outside your comfort zone. You assume you will not enjoy your date? Go anyway. You have nothing to lose. You think that you wouldn't enjoy playing tennis. Try it anyway. Act differently and notice the different outcomes and experiences this brings into your life. Take a risk.

Catastrophizing

When you catastrophize you take a smallish situation and blow it out of all proportion so that you imagine all sorts of dreadful things happening as a result of it. You magnify or exaggerate the importance of things that you have caused or the achievements or qualities of others. Alongside this goes minimizing, where you shrink the importance of positive things to assume a negative outcome.

Examples of catastrophizing

• *You spill something on your clothes just before you go to a party. You assume that everyone will mock you.*

• *Your girlfriend fails to turn up for a date. You assume that either this is her way of telling you the relationship is over or perhaps she has been run over. You create pictures in your mind of ever-greater disastrous scenarios.*

• *You magnify a personal shortcoming: 'I've put on three pounds in weight. I am the fattest person in the world. I can't meet my friends!'*

• *You minimize a positive attribute: you set out for a party, assuming that it will be a disaster because you aren't interesting enough, ignoring the fact that you have a great sense of humour that could mean that you have a lot of fun there.*

Problems with catastrophizing

You assume the worst possible result. You only imagine the worst scenario or an extremely negative outcome. If the smallest circumstance or event has the potential to be magnified in a negative way, it will cause you negative emotions as well as restricting the actions you take. For example, you may feed feelings of low self-esteem, anxiety or depression. The smallest disagreement becomes the end of a relationship, a mistake becomes a great failure and a shortcoming becomes your whole identity.

How to challenge catastrophizing

1 **Get some perspective**. Stop your catastrophic thinking as soon as you spot it. Does what happened *really* have to lead to a

must know

Ten main types of faulty thinking:
6. Catastrophizing – either by magnification, i.e. exaggerating the importance of things, or by minimizing, i.e. underemphasizing the importance of aspects of a situation.

disaster? So you spilt something on your clothes. Most people have probably done the same at some time. Did anyone even notice? And does it matter?

2 What resources do you have? Notice what resources you have – in terms of people and personal qualities – to change your attitude to the situation you are in so that you prevent it from escalating and becoming a self-fulfilling prophecy.

3 Do your personal shortcomings really affect the bigger picture? Look at the facts and evidence. Will the particular shortcoming that you have identified really affect your ability to achieve the major things you want in your life?

4 Experiment. What would happen if you were to ignore a shortcoming and concentrate on another personal quality instead? What strengths can you identify that you also have? Could these outweigh your shortcomings in this particular situation?

5 Remember you have learnt and changed before. You can do it again. Time cures many situations. You have survived difficult or embarrassing situations in the past. Focus on how strong you are in reality.

Emotional reasoning

Emotional reasoning is the assumption that your negative emotions are a true reflection of the state of things. If you rely on negative feelings to guide you, you can set up a vicious circle of escalating negativity or pessimism. As you become convinced your feelings must have a basis, you look for other things to become negative about. Your mindset becomes hardened into a more negative setting.

Examples of emotional reasoning

• *You haven't been sleeping well because of noise outside your window at night. You feel less tolerant of people around you and more irritable because you are tired. You are given a problem to deal with at work. You assume that your colleagues are being more unhelpful than usual when in fact it is simply your tiredness making you believe their actions have a different significance from normal.*

• *You feel jealous when you see your partner with his ex-girlfriend at a party. Because you feel jealous, you assume that has to mean your partner really is still in love with her.*

Problems with emotional reasoning

• **Emotions are not facts**. If you rely on your emotions to be your guide it takes you away from the evidence of what is happening in a particular situation. For example, just because you feel jealous that your wife goes dancing with a good-looking friend does not mean that you need to be jealous.

• **Emotions can be triggered by physical tiredness**. We are not always aware of what triggers certain emotions. It is dangerous to interpret emotions as necessarily being directly caused by one particular event.

How to challenge emotional reasoning

1. **Identify your emotional reasoning**. How precisely are you feeling? Separate the feeling out from the cause you think you have identified. For example, 'I am feeling depressed because she hasn't rung me and so if I am depressed it means she doesn't love me'. Recognize instead the possibility

must know

Ten main types of faulty thinking:
7. Emotional reasoning – you assume your negative emotions reflect the way things really are.

must know

Ten main types of faulty thinking:
8. Labelling and mislabelling – using inaccurate and emotive language to describe an event.

that your feelings are triggered by your emotional state rather than an indication of the facts of the situation.

2. Notice the difference between what you would normally think about a situation and how your mood is affecting your thinking. Ask yourself, 'When I am not feeling negative (upset, afraid, angry, jealous, depressed, etc.) do I think the same way about this situation?'

3. Get perspective after the event. After you have let go of the peak of the emotion, think about the situation again. How do you view it now? What fresh perspective do you have on yourself and the situation?

Labelling and mislabelling

Irrational labelling is when we give a label to something which limits our thinking about ourselves or other people. We need to label things as a normal part of our everyday communication. However, if the label becomes all we see or hear about a situation or person we stop looking at the facts and just go by our prejudices.

Language clues
• *I am just so stupid, fat, unattractive.*
• *He's just an alcoholic.*
• *She's a typical estate agent/lawyer.*
• *I am a person who is always making mistakes.*
• *He is a horrible person – he always forgets to call.*
• *It's a dangerous world out there.*

Examples of labelling
• *You fail your first driving test. You are so disappointed that you label yourself a failure.*

• *You fall over at a party and someone laughs. You label them as a horrible person. You don't make an effort to be friends with them as a result.*
• *You hear about a robbery in your neighbourhood. You label your area as a crime-ridden, dangerous place to live. You worry every time you go out and leave your house empty.*

Problems with labelling
• Labelling yourself as useless or as stupid may cause you to beat yourself up emotionally.
• Labelling others may cause you to have negative feelings towards them.
• Labelling the world around you in a negative way may stop you taking risks.

How to challenge labelling
1. **Remember that you are fallible**. A person's identity is more than their behaviour or the name they are given. Distinguish between what someone does and who they are. A mistake doesn't make someone stupid. A person who practises law is more in their life than just a lawyer. The danger of labelling someone even with their job title is that it might lead you to assume the absence of other skills, e.g. he is a lawyer so he must be rubbish at plumbing.
2. **Consider other aspects of a situation or person**. Labelling can cause you to overgeneralize or indulge in all-or-nothing thinking (see pages 27–9). We are all complex individuals with different degrees of ability in one area or another. One negative event or personal characteristic doesn't have to lead to a negative label. Challenge your thinking by allowing space that there might be more to people and things than this simple view of them.

Irrational 'should', 'must', 'ought to', 'have to' statements

Examples of should, must, ought to, have to statements

* *He should help me – he's my son.*
* *She should have paid more attention to me. All wives need to listen to their husbands.*
* *I must do that job. I have no choice.*
* *I have to have respect.*
* *You must not steal money.*
* *I have to work hard. I don't have a choice.*

must know

Ten main types of faulty thinking:
9. 'Should', 'must', 'ought to' and 'have to' statements result in guilt about yourself, or feelings of resentment, anger and frustration towards others.

Problems with should, must, ought to, have to thinking

* **Rigidity and moralistic rules**: The word 'should' is an indication of a personal rule or demand. If you violate this rule it implies there are negative consequences for the person who has made the statement. These rules or commands are often moral or societal. The use of 'should' and 'have to' statements implies that they are absolute and so limits the speaker's flexibility of action and thought.
* **Guilt, resentment, frustration and anger**: Using this type of statement causes us to point a finger mentally at whoever breaks rules. If we are angry with someone else – 'she should have helped me' – we will point the finger at them. If we break our own rules we will point a finger inwards which causes either self-anger or guilt.
* **It's not magic**: These statements imply a belief in magic rather than reality. 'I do something and the result should be the exact one I predict'. This is essentially an irrational way of looking at the world because it assumes that the circumstances will

always be the same every time the rule is applied. In real life a variety of factors may change an outcome in each new situation. For example, 'The shop should sell bread. Why isn't it here?'. In reality, the shop wants to sell bread but one day a delivery fails to arrive. If you don't recognize that circumstances may change, you will end up feeling angry about situations.

• **It's your choice:** When you use 'have to' statements you are assuming that there is someone or something forcing you to do something you don't want to do. If you are being held at gunpoint then you 'have to' do it. Otherwise you are making a choice and a decision to do it. It may feel like a 'have to' because there may be unpleasant consequences if you make a choice *not to*. However, it is still a choice. For example, 'I have to go to work'. Actually no you don't. If you don't, you may have no money but you are still making a choice. The choice you are making is simply the better alternative.

How to challenge should, must, ought to, have to thinking

1. **Recognize rules as preferences**: By recognizing that your shoulds and musts are just preferences, you can free yourself to be more adaptable to circumstances as they arrive. Of course, many of your rules may be useful recommended practices. At the same time, it can be helpful if you question your rules. Must this be true? What would happen if it wasn't? Where did this belief come from? What would it be like if I didn't hold this belief?

2. **Accept current reality**: In accepting that reality is as it is, the benefit is that you are freed up to

---

must know

Ten main types of faulty thinking:
10. Personalization and blame – you see yourself as the cause of some negative external event.

respond to the circumstances as they are rather than as you think they 'should be'. Look at and respond to the 'real' ingredients of the situation rather than those you want to be there. For example, 'She shouldn't get angry with me for being late'. If she has shouted at you, that's not going to disappear just because you think it should be different. What can you do to respond to what has happened?

3. Deal with your anger: Anger serves no useful purpose other than to alert us to our personal rules. Your desire for change won't be helped by it, so you might as well accept the situation as it is. When you can look at things calmly and notice your beliefs, you are seeing reality. You are then in a good position to decide what actions you can take that will help you.

4. Change your 'have to's to 'choosing to's: Remember, you don't have to do anything unless you are being physically overwhelmed. Otherwise it is a choice. Do you prefer the consequences of choosing to or not choosing to?

5. Change irrational 'shoulds' to wishes: Changing your should statements to wishes gives you more flexibility for movement in your response to a situation. For example:

Change: 'She shouldn't speak to me like that'.

To: 'I wish she would speak to me with more respect but at the moment she doesn't. What can I do to encourage her to speak to me in a different way?'

Change: 'I should have done that job better.'

To: 'I wish I had done that job better, but I didn't. What could I do next time that would get a better result? How could I prepare differently?'

Personalization and blame

When you personalize, you inaccurately see yourself as the cause of some negative external event or blame someone or something else for a situation they have not caused or they have only in part caused.

Examples of personalization and blame
• *My husband is stressed. It must be because of me.*
• *If I had been a good mother my son wouldn't have got divorced.*

Problems with personalization and blame
• **Anger and resentment towards others**. If you think a situation has been caused 100 per cent by someone else it will create anger.
• **Guilt**. Seeing yourself as the cause results in guilt, as well as negative self-talk and self-anger.
• **Inaccurate solutions**. Rather than addressing the situation as it really is, you attempt to find a solution to a cause that doesn't exist. It's as if you had baked a cake that had come out of the oven flat. When you make the next one, you add more butter when the real problem is that you used plain flour rather than self-raising.

How to challenge personalization and blame
1. **Gather information**. Often personalization and blame are rooted in misinformation or lack of information. This makes people jump to conclusions about the cause of an unpleasant situation. Our thoughts are responsible for our behaviour. Other people's thoughts are responsible for their behaviour. Usually conflict is caused by a miscommunication and/or a number of decisions influencing the outcome.
2. **Recognize the world does not revolve around you**. Other people have their own motivations, their own view of the world and their own responsibilities. You are not the core of the world around which everything revolves. This absolves you of any need to be the cause of everything around you!

Confusing 'want to' with 'need to'
Confusing our wants with our needs is one of the most general types of faulty thinking. Absolute needs do indeed exist. These

must know

Ten more types of faulty thinking:
11. Confusing 'want to' with 'need to'.
12. Worrying as a preventative measure – thinking that by worrying you will stop a negative outcome.
13. Irrational definitions – having rigid definitions of concepts.
14. Projection – assuming that the beliefs you hold must be held by others.
15. Hopeless/helpless thinking – assuming that there is no solution to a problem and you are helpless.
16. Too much or too little thinking.
17. Turning predictions into probabilities – thinking that just because an outcome may occur, it necessarily will occur.
18. Confusing 'not able' with 'won't'.
19. Attachment to irrational ideas.
20. Confusing 'rely' with 'depend'.

are the basics that we as human beings need to exist – food, air and water. Everything else is a want – something we have decided is vitally important to us. Confusion arises when we or others refer to these as needs, as can be seen in the well-known model called Abraham Maslow's Hierarchy of Needs (see box, page 48).

Language clues
• *I need to*
• *I can't stand it*

Examples of false needs
These are often referred to as needs when they are actually wants.
• *love*
• *attention*
• *education*
• *money*
• *respect*
• *health*
• *perfection*
• *success*
• *being liked*
• *self-esteem*
• *an easy life*
• *possessions*
• *rights*

Problems with need statements
• **Anger, anxiety and resentment**. As with 'ought to' statements, 'need' statements can cause anger, resentment or anxiety. Your partner tells you that he/she doesn't respect or love you. If you 'need' this

from them you will feel angry. The train is late. If you need it to be on time, you will panic. However, now contrast this to an actual need. What would you be feeling if you were told you would have no water for several days?

• **Labelling love as a need**. Most people want love and many may think that they need love but this does not make it a need rather than a want. Unlike air, water and food, we can survive without it. Importantly, if we define love we will all have our personal rules about what love is, each definition being composed of personal wants. For example, tenderness, hugging, time spent together, saying that they love me, etc.

• **Conditional needs**. Sometimes we make statements that imply a series of conditions needs to be met. For example, 'I need a nice house to make me happy.' The problem with this is that the person will act in accordance with this rule as if this is an absolute rule; if their conditions are not met, there will be a negative result for the person who has made the rule. They may feel unhappy, angry or mislabel themselves a failure.

How to challenge 'need' statements

1. **Changing your 'need' statements to 'want to's**. Recognize the difference between wants and the absolute needs that we as human beings have. When you catch yourself saying 'need to', change your statement to 'want to'.

2. **Will you live?** Ask yourself, will I live without this? How long could you go without your perceived 'need' without dying? If you can survive as a human being it is a want. Note also that even if a person kills

Maslow's Hierarchy of Needs

Abraham Maslow produced a model in 1954 suggesting six sets of goals that would lead to a happy and satisfied life.

- physiological,
- safety,
- love,
- esteem,
- aesthetic and cognitive
- self-actualization or self-fulfilment.

He arranged these into different levels in order of importance, as follows.

The basic needs are hunger, thirst and sleep. When these are satisfied they are replaced by safety needs. Next come the need to love – to belong to a group and to give and receive friendship. When these are satisfied there are esteem needs: a need for self-esteem and respect, recognition and appreciation. When these are satisfied, there is room for an appreciation of knowledge and the aesthetic. Then finally there is a need for self-fulfilment and self-actualization.

From a CBT standpoint, only the basic needs are actual needs. The others may be desirable but are not essential.

him or herself, it is not the lack of the want doing the killing – it is the person who decides to take their life.

3. Change your 'can't stand it's to 'wants'. 'Can't stand it' is another way of expressing a 'need to'. It presumes that a situation is so intolerable that you don't have a choice in experiencing it – you need the situation to be different. To dispute this, recognize that it is a want. Change 'I can't stand her treating me like a child' to 'I don't like her treating me like a child and because of this I am going to tell her so or leave now.'

Worrying as a preventative measure

Worry is when we think obsessively about something that we fear or don't want to happen in the future. Often what we worry about does not come true. Some people may make a link between the fact that they have worried and a more positive outcome has resulted to conclude falsely that the worrying was the cause of a positive outcome. This is also sometimes referred to as 'magical worry'.

Examples of worrying as a preventative measure

• *If I worry about the train being late, it will be on time.*
• *If I think about the airline losing my baggage and plan for the possibility, it will probably never happen.*

Problems with worrying as a preventative measure

• **False actions**. Thinking obsessively about your future may make you think you are taking actions towards a better outcome when in fact you are doing nothing.
• **Voodoo/talisman thinking**: Negative thoughts cannot cause a positive outcome. If you have a concern and just think about it rather than take action to prevent it from occurring you are not doing anything to create more positive events in your life. All you are doing is using worry as a form of false voodoo or a talisman to prevent you from coming to any harm.

How to challenge worrying as a preventative measure

1. **Replace your worries with actions**. Recognize that worry is a false protection. It cannot stop bad things happening to you or

make good things happen. However, taking actions to change an outcome really may result in a positive result. When you come across a concern, act on it rather than worry.

2. Gather information. If you are worried, decide what you want and gather the information and facts available to you. This way you can decide whether your fear is false or true – whether or not you are faced with a real threat. Make your prediction based on the facts available to you and take decisive action to cut off the future you will worry about.

Irrational definitions

An irrational definition is when we take an important concept or value such as 'love' and define it in a way that gives us little flexibility. In other words our personal rules or 'complex equivalents' for what 'love' means are narrow or rigid and so ultimately limiting and disempowering.

Examples of irrational definitions

• *He doesn't give me presents or pay for me when we go out, so he doesn't love me.*
• *I am a failure because my classmates have all gone on to have better careers than me.*
• *I would have to be able to have children to be a success as a woman.*
• *My child never tidies up so he is lazy.*

Problems with irrational definitions

Self-defeating. Irrational definitions are self-defeating. They are rigid and so leave us very little room for the complexity of life, human reactions and flexibility in our responses to a situation.

How to challenge irrational definitions

1. Recognize your core beliefs and assess whether they work for you. Irrational definitions come out of core beliefs and values we hold about the world that are generally unconscious.

Listen to your language and challenge your rigid definitions or concepts. Notice that many of them may lead to an all-or-nothing, good/bad approach to life.

2. Replace 'black and white' thinking with 'sometimes' thinking. For example, change 'I am not a success/successful because I don't have children,' to 'I am a normal human being who has certain things in my life that make me happy and some that don't'. 'I am not totally successful or totally unsuccessful. There are degrees of both and they are neither good nor bad.'

Projection

Projection is a form of mind reading. It is the assumption that the beliefs and thoughts we hold must also tend to be held by other people and therefore the actions they would take would be the same as those we would take in the same circumstances.

Examples of projection

• *I believe that I am a failure so when the audience looks at me when I present to them they must believe it too because it is so clear I am a failure.*

• *I am fat and therefore unattractive. Society believes that fat people are ugly so it is obvious the majority of men will look at me and not find me desirable.*

• *I wouldn't hand in money if I found it in the street. It is likely that other people would not either.*

• *My friends and I always gossip. It's normal, isn't it?*

• *I might be tempted to sleep with someone else or lie when I am married, so my partner probably will too.*

Problems with projection

Different models of the world. Each of us has a different map or model of the world: a different way of looking at things formed by differing beliefs and values. When we project, we assume our own motivations and beliefs are generally held by others. This can lead us to attribute our views of ourselves to other people and to assume that they will do what we would do in the same circumstances. If you project and your self-view is negative, you will project negatively onto others.

How to challenge projection

1. Remember your assumption may be a projection. If you gossip about others it doesn't mean they will gossip about you. Just because you have a poor self-image, it does not mean other people will view you in the same way. Because you think that society holds certain beliefs, it does not mean that everyone in society does. Ask yourself, 'Am I just thinking that they will think like that because I would tend to think like that in the same circumstances?'

Hopeless/helpless thinking

Hopeless or helpless thinking assumes that a problem exists, information has been gathered but a solution cannot be found; therefore a solution does not exist and cannot exist in the future. This type of thinking comes from deeply held beliefs about the world and ourselves. Sometimes it has been learnt as a result of a person taking on board the expertise of another person who has voiced a strong opinion about a subject. The helpless thinker adopts this expert voice as a core belief and acts in accordance with it for many years afterwards.

Examples of hopeless/ helpless thinking
• *I'll never be a success.*
• *I will never get married.*
• *Other people do well but I never do.*

Problems with hopeless/helpless thinking
• **Unconscious assumptions of failure**: Hopeless/helpless thinking is learned thinking. We start out in life often believing

that anything is possible. Then we learn – either by hearing or observing others – to believe that we cannot succeed in some aspect of our lives. This becomes an unconscious belief that results in an automatic assumption of failure. It then becomes self-fulfilling if it is not challenged since you are unlikely to take actions towards a goal you want if you believe you are automatically doomed to failure.

• **Anger**. Sometimes helpless thinking not only *causes* people to give up but also *results* from having given up too early. If you are an impatient person you may not be willing to spend the time needed to make a 'want' into a result. Or if you do not know how to recognize blocks and obstacles as something that can be worked through rather than as something scary or dreadful you may give up prematurely, feeling frustrated and angry with yourself and others. The result is a feeling of being helpless to overcome setbacks through effort.

How to challenge helpless/hopeless thinking

1. Question the experts. Because a figure of authority/expert once told you something it doesn't mean it is necessarily true, true for all time or true in all contexts. An expert is only expressing an opinion that may have *some* evidence behind it. If you don't like what you are being told, question the evidence. Go out and find counter-examples. Research and look for other options and opportunities that will allow you to get the goal you want. Use your logic to analyse the information you obtain and see what alternative routes may be possible.

2. View setbacks as feedback. When you hit an obstacle be careful to use it as an opportunity to gather information rather than treating it as a permanent failure point. This is the most useful way to think if you want to achieve anything that will take effort.

3. Remember that you are unique. Just because no one else has achieved what you want to achieve it doesn't exclude you from success. Just because other people say it is impossible it doesn't make it so. There are many examples in history of people who disprove the majority. If it is possible for a human being to do what you want to do then research and see how you could be successful.

Too much/too little thinking

This type of thinking makes the assumption that you will fail to reach the outcome you want because you have too much or too little of a particular quality or behaviour.

Examples of too much/too little thinking

- *I'm too stupid.*
- *I'm too unattractive.*
- *He is too fat.*
- *She is too dirty.*
- *He doesn't wash enough.*
- *She eats too much.*

Problems with too much/too little thinking

Loss of your goal. Someone who talks in too much/too little terms has lost their outcome. The statement 'I'm too stupid', for example, implies that in the speaker's mind their self-view is a block to obtaining an outcome, but what outcome? 'I'm too stupid' to be, have or do what? If you can identify what outcome you want then you can start looking at your self-view as a practical problem that might have a solution.

How to challenge too much/too little thinking

1. **Ask the question 'For what/ for what purpose?'**. When you ask this question, the speaker is forced to relate their too much/too little statements to an outcome. For example, 'I am too stupid to get the degree I want.' As soon as you have the goal, you potentially have the means of achieving it. You can

look rationally at what you believe to be the obstacle to achieving the goal and decide whether it is an issue and, if it is, what you can do to get rid of it.

For example, 'Let me look at how much study it would take for me to achieve the degree I want. Maybe I will have to study harder and for more hours than other people. What would happen if I were to experiment and see the results of studying harder?'

Confusing 'not able' with 'won't'

A person who 'cannot' do something because of lack of skills, knowledge or other abilities is not the same as someone who does not have the motivation and is not willing to make the choice to do it.

Examples of confusing 'not able' with 'won't'
- *I can't go on a blind date.*
- *I can't say no to my boss.*
- *I can't ask for a salary increase.*
- *I can't break up with my girlfriend.*
- *I can't make presentations in front of an audience.*

Problems with confusing 'not able' with 'won't'
Fear, discomfort and anxiety. The word 'can't' in the English language is used both to imply a lack of mental or physical skills and a refusal to do something. When it is used in the latter sense it suggests that the speaker feels a lack of choice. In fact they do have a choice and have simply assessed that the consequences of making the choice are worse than those of not making it. For example, in the speaker's mind saying 'no' might have more scary consequences than saying nothing.

Not asking for a salary increase may result in long-term loss of money but short-term no loss of face if the request were to be refused.

How to challenge confusing 'not able' with 'won't'

1. Learn how to do something new in a comfortable way.

If you are stopping yourself from carrying out a particular behaviour, it is because you are afraid of the negative and uncomfortable feelings that may result from it. You may know how to take the action – just not how to take it in a comfortable way. Ask yourself whether you have the basic mental or physical abilities, skills or knowledge to do the action at all. If the answer is yes then you 'can' take an action, you simply feel uncomfortable doing it at the moment. For example, 'I feel uncomfortable giving presentations at the moment. What could I learn to make this a more enjoyable/comfortable experience?'

Attachment to irrational 'ideas'

Sometimes people become upset because they have latched onto a particular idea/belief that they have learned is supposed to be negative. They ignore the facts as to whether it does indeed have negative consequences for them and assume it will. Because they have been taught that this circumstance will cause a problem, they assume it does until challenged. These may be instances where a person has adopted core beliefs about him or herself thanks to the influence of an 'expert voice' – someone in authority telling them that a situation will inevitably lead to a problem outcome.

Examples of attachment to irrational ideas
• *Being obese*
• *Being 'too' thin*

- *Becoming 50*
- *Being bald*
- *Having a large nose*
- *Having small breasts*
- *Being very tall or short*
- *Having people dislike you*
- *Being single*
- *Getting grey hair young*
- *Having a large scar or birthmark*

Problems with attachment to irrational ideas

Upset. When a person is attached to an irrational idea they assume that it is a block or obstacle. You may hear them say something like, 'I am too short' or 'I am 50 years old.' But when they are challenged to articulate what problems they have had in reaching goals because they are too short they may not be able to point to any real examples. They have simply been taught to expect this to be a problem. Often an attachment to an irrational idea can then become a block or excuse for not setting goals.

How to challenge attachment to irrational ideas

Find out the facts. When a person is attached to an idea, it is important to challenge them by assessing the real facts. 'Where specifically has it been a problem for you being 50/ too short? Do you think that this has caused you a practical problem in obtaining a goal or have you simply been told that it is supposed to be a problem?'

want to know more?

• For interesting online materials look at www.reflectivehappiness.com
• *Learned Optimism: How to Change Your Mind and Your Life* by Martin E. P. Seligman
• Chapter 5 explains how to use your ABC sheets to identify automatic thoughts.
• Chapters 7 to 11 look at faulty thinking in depression, anger, anxiety, stress and self-esteem.

3 The foundation of change

This chapter looks at how the basic principles of CBT can be used to create real and lasting change. You will learn about unhelpful beliefs you may currently hold that block change and discover some helpful beliefs that aid change.

The foundation of change

For many people change is about avoiding or reducing emotional and psychological disorders. If you have tried to avoid distress in the past, paradoxically you may have only reinforced your fears about relapsing into further distress.

must know

How to re-programme your habits

1. Identify what you don't want any more – behaviour, feelings and automatic thoughts.
2. Identify new helpful thoughts.
3. Practise new habits - behaviour, feeling and thoughts. Accept some discomfort or disbelief in these new habits.
4. Continue to practise new habits - behaviour, feeling and thoughts.
5. New habits become unconscious and automatic.

Permanent change

Permanent change to your emotional response to different events is possible with CBT. Using the tools in the next few chapters, you will learn how to change your emotional frames of reference and make real changes to your automatic thoughts and state of mind.

As with all change, re-educating your emotions will only happen if you practise. Practice makes conscious change become unconscious and permanent. When you practise taking a rational approach to your fears and worries, you will understand how to undo the triggers to your negative and counterproductive feelings.

As already said, in CBT, you can work by yourself or with a therapist. Remember, whether you work by yourself or with someone else you are still in control of your results.

This chapter outlines the general principles to follow to create change. To put these principles into practice, proceed to the next chapter and start to fill out the worksheets.

Learning new habits and skills

How you move from not being able to do something to being able to do something is shown in the competence model below. There are four levels of change in learning (see also pages 62–3):

Unconscious incompetence
Conscious incompetence
Conscious competence
Unconscious competence

When you practise something for the first time it probably feels uncomfortable. After a while it becomes more comfortable, and gradually it becomes an automatic action. There are lots of examples of things in your life you once couldn't do and now you can.

For example, do you remember what it was like to learn to tie your shoelaces or to tell the time or to read? Do you drive? If you do, you have learned a very complex set of behaviours and reactions through practice.

These are skills that at one point in your life you couldn't do and now can. Perhaps you can think of other examples of how you have changed your behaviours and reactions to situations through practice? Maybe at one point in your life you used to feel nervous when you made a work call or presentation and now you don't. Perhaps you felt a little worried the first time you kissed your current partner and now you feel relaxed with them? At one time you didn't know how to buy something online, now you may be very calm about using the internet for shopping.

We face new situations all the time. If we keep practising new and helpful thoughts about them we become more and more used to reacting in positive

must know

Habit forming
Identifying your unwanted habits comes from your conscious intellect. However, habit forming takes place at an unconscious level through practice.

ways when these situations occur. Identify your faulty thinking and practise new thoughts.

How we learn and change
New habits and changing existing habits take root at the unconscious level. It is not a case of just telling yourself 'I must change' or 'I will change'. When you identify and challenge your thoughts, and then practise the new ones, you are re-programming (re-educating) yourself to trigger new habits of thought, behaviour and feeling.

The four stages of competence

Stage one: unconscious incompetence
When you start to make a change, you are (blissfully) ignorant about what you need to change and how to change it. You can't do the new habit yet, but you are also unconscious of this.

Stage two: conscious incompetence
Remember what it was like the very first time you decided to learn a new skill? You suddenly realized the big gap between what you could do and what you wanted to do. When you are consciously incompetent, you become aware of your own lack of mastery in the habit you want to learn. If you are using CBT to identify goals you want to achieve, this stage will probably happen at the point at which you have begun to identify your irrational beliefs and to realize which faulty thinking patterns you are using.

Stage three: conscious competence
As you first start to learn new ways of doing things, of thinking and of feeling, you are still aware that you

are learning. You may experience what is known as cognitive-emotional dissonance – a gap between your thoughts and feelings. You understand that you have made progress and that you have acquired some skills compared to stage one. At the same time, your skills are not yet automatic and so, understandably, may not yet feel totally natural.

Stage four: unconscious competence
At this stage you acquire mastery of the new skills you set out to learn. After you have practised and practised, your new habits or new skills will become totally automatic, unconscious and feel natural. You become competent at the new habit or skill and, at the same time, you have become so good at doing it that at the point you become competent, you are not aware of just how competent you now are. The beliefs that underlie your new habits have become deeply embedded. For example, once upon a time you would have thought of yourself as someone who was a non-reader. Now you believe that you are a reader. If you once smoked you would have thought of yourself as a smoker. Now you think of yourself as a non-smoker. The new beliefs become part of your unconscious identity.

must know

General goal-setting questions
• What do I want in my life?
• What gives me pleasure and enjoyment?
• What would I like to change?
• What would I wish for instead?

The stages of change
It is important to be systematic and consistent in how you apply CBT if you want to achieve lasting change. The stages of the CBT approach are given below and the worksheets for each stage are given in Chapter 4. Extra exercises and worksheets are given in the third part of the book, looking at specific emotional disorders such as depression and anxiety.

must know

Seven steps to create permanent change
1. Assess your starting point. What do you want to change? Develop a problem list.
2. Set goals. What do you want to have less of and more of in your life?
3. Uncover and identify irrational thoughts and beliefs. Recognize that these thoughts are creating unwanted feelings.
4. Develop new rational thoughts as a replacement. Practise your new way of thinking and refuse to entertain the old thoughts any more. Recognize that even though the new thoughts don't feel real yet, they may in the future.
5. 'Act as if' you do believe the new thoughts until they become automatic thoughts.
6. Practise and practise again!
7. Keep a record and self-monitor your progress.

Step one: assess where you are now

CBT is similar to a coaching process in that, if you are working with a therapist, he or she will probably carry out an assessment of your current situation. This will take place at the beginning of your therapy and also at the beginning of subsequent sessions.

The easiest way to start if you are working by yourself is to write a problem list – what you want to get rid of in your life. For example:

• *I am constantly worried about losing my job.*
• *I am stressed because I have two small children.*
• *I am anxious that my wife will leave me because I am getting so down every week.*
• *We are finding it more and more difficult to communicate effectively.*
• *She is eating too much and putting on weight and I am not finding her attractive in the same way as I used to, which isn't helping our relationship either.*
• *Money is tight, which is making me more stressed.*
• *Recently I have had two panic attacks.*

Step two: set goals for your therapy

Next, decide what your goals are. When you feel overpowered by emotions, initially it may not be easy to separate yourself from them and set objective goals. If this is the case, be gentle in your goal setting. You can set yourself more stretching goals as you go on.

The overall aim of CBT is clear: to change the response (B – beliefs/thoughts and C – consequences/emotions/behaviour) you currently have in reaction to trigger situations (A – activating events). By dealing with these reactions you will learn to respond automatically in a rational and appropriate way to particular situations with the help of tools that you can use at any time in the future.

You will also have your own individual goals which will be very specific. They are probably a mix of problems you want to avoid and what you would like instead.

Learn to turn problems into goals. For example, the problem you start off with might be something like 'I get depressed because I am not good at relationships' or 'I am nervous of flying'.

You can turn these problems into goals by thinking about what you want to have in your life instead – this will be a mix of feelings, thoughts and behaviours.

If you are working with a therapist, it is still up to you to say what you want. A therapist will not tell you what you 'should' think or feel. Coming up with clear goals is very important as they will become your motivation and reason for pursuing the practice of changing your thoughts, beliefs and assumptions about events.

The goal sheets in the next chapter will give you a structure for this task.

Step three: get to know your faulty thinking patterns and beliefs

If you have ever been to an old-fashioned circus or even a zoo you have probably seen a fully grown elephant tethered by a small chain. You may have wondered why these huge creatures don't break their shackles. It is clear that any adult elephant could easily break free in a moment, yet they don't.

The strange thing is that the baby elephants often have stronger chains than the older, bigger ones. The reason is that the older ones learnt when they were young that they couldn't escape and so as they grew up, they just accepted that the chains would hold them and ceased to struggle, even though they were becoming stronger and stronger. The baby elephants still pull at the chain or try to uproot the stake they are tied to until they give up.

A prisoner of his beliefs has given up because he thinks what he learnt in the past is still true. Our beliefs can be as strong a constraint on our behaviour as that tiny chain is for the adult elephant. If you want to change, you need to break those chains and be as strongly motivated as the baby elephant is to have its freedom.

By challenging your beliefs – even core beliefs – your self-talk, automatic thoughts and the meaning you attach to situations will change.

Step four: begin to develop new rational beliefs

The way to change thoughts is to dispute and disprove the beliefs you no longer want. If you hold certain beliefs to be true, your brain will actively filter for evidence to keep proving them. To modify your thoughts, the best way is to search out counter-examples and evidence of times when the belief is disproved.

Use the lists in Chapter 2 to identify any types of faulty thinking you are using and challenge these with new, more rational and helpful beliefs.

Step five: 'act as if'

Cognitive behavioural therapy is a process of experimentation. Identify the ways of thinking, being or doing you want to get rid of and try out new ones until you get the results that make you happy. Be prepared to act in new ways – in other words, 'act as if'.

'Acting as if' means that you take a hypothesis – a new belief – and you experiment to see what would happen if you really held this belief.

By acting as if you believe something new, you will experience new behaviours and new thoughts about yourself, and there will be new emotional and physical consequences. If you enjoy the outcome of holding this new hypothetical belief then you will start to build it as a genuine belief and undermine, modify or destroy the original disempowering or unhelpful belief.

Step six: repeat and practice

Change comes through practice, which will enable you to form new habits of thinking, acting and feeling. Practising new beliefs and actions will help you to learn how to do things in a new way and, importantly, how to conduct your new behaviours in a way that feels both comfortable and familiar.

Step seven: self-monitor

Self-monitoring is a key stage of change. It means observing the changes you are making to your thoughts and feelings.

It is important to measure your mood when you begin a CBT programme as this will allow you to check your progress and set new goals (see Mood diary in Chapter 5). If you are working by yourself you can do this by dating your worksheets and noting down on each one how you feel.

Also keep a check on your level of conviction in your old faulty beliefs and your new rational ones to see how that changes.

Over several weeks, you will be able to track your progress and notice your emotional improvement, as well as the belief changes you make.

One useful tool for self-monitoring is to keep a record of your changing ABC sheets (see Chapter 5). You can also use a diary or notebook to write down patterns of thoughts and activities. By recording changes, you will see the methods that work best for you and also have conscious proof of the changes you are making.

What results should I expect from CBT?

Change re-educates your thinking patterns to produce more positive and neutral thoughts and emotions and fewer negative ones.

Some people get confused about what a useful goal for change would feel like. If they are accustomed to experiencing strong negative emotions, they assume that they need to experience a strong positive emotion as proof that the old negative one has gone. A feeling does not have to be a strong feeling to be worth experiencing. A calm, neutral feeling is still a feeling and as much the opposite of a negative feeling as a strong positive one.

Opposite are three different ABC scenarios you may experience as the result of creating change. One is not comfortable to experience. Either of the other two would show that you had created comfortable change.

must know

From a thought to a feeling
• Negative thoughts produce negative emotions
• Positive thoughts produce positive emotions.
• Neutral thoughts produce neutral emotions.

Unhelpful and irrational beliefs

These are commonly held beliefs that are unhelpful if you want to create change and some thoughts to change them.

1. Approval is a necessity, i.e. you need to be loved by other people for everything you do. Instead think about focusing on self-respect and being a living person rather than someone who 'has to be loved' or 'needs' approval.

2. Some people are awful and do terrible, wicked things. No matter how terrible the thing they have done, there is a reason for it. Instead of condemning an individual for what he or she does, separate the behaviour from the person. A person's

Negative ABC

A – activating event	B – beliefs, thoughts	C – consequences
'I don't want this marriage any more.'	'He/she doesn't love me. I am unlovable. There will never be anyone like him/her. This was my last chance. I can't carry on.'	'I feel terrible. I feel depressed, I hate myself. I must try to win her/him back.'

Positive ABC

A – activating event	B – beliefs , thoughts	C – consequences
'I don't want this marriage any more.'	'I wasn't happy in this marriage either. The fact that he/she says it is over means that I am free. It's great, I was looking for a way out. Now I have one.'	'I feel free and happy and exhilarated. I can't wait to say goodbye and move on!'

Neutral ABC

A- activating event	B – beliefs , thoughts	C – consequences
'I don't want this marriage any more.'	'I wanted this marriage to work but we have both tried and he/she has made up his/her mind. I am going to miss all that we had together but we had good times and I can create good times in the future with another partner. I still have the rest of my life to lead.'	'I can move on. I feel calm and ready for the next stage. I will be OK. You will be OK.'

behaviour does not make him a 'bad' person. It could be more useful to think that the person (maybe you?) is behaving in an unhelpful, stupid or self-defeating fashion. If you feel mistreated, or other people feel mistreated by you, the most useful thing to do is to see as many perspectives as possible on the issue, discuss what has happened and find ways to put things right. Blame just creates two losers.

3. You are a suffering victim of external events. This belief is based on the idea that misery is forced upon people by external circumstances and events, i.e. we are not able to cause the circumstances in our lives. A more useful and empowering belief is that unhappiness is caused by the meaning we give to circumstances and events.

4. When things aren't how you want them to be, they are 'bad' and it is 'horrible'. This belief has the idea of finality and permanence within it. Instead it is more useful to see that you are experiencing bad conditions that you can change by choosing to react to them in a different way.

5. If something is frightening you need to obsess about it. It is pointless to waste energy thinking obsessively about potentially dangerous or fearful situations. It is better to face them full on and come up with options for getting rid of the aspects that worry you. If you find that it not possible at that point you can accept the situation as it is.

6. You need to be perfect. It is pointless striving to be totally successful, intelligent or any other quality. Accept that you and every other person on earth is imperfect and fallible.

7. You need to have certainty. The world is full of uncertainty and risk. The idea that we have to control all risk and get rid of all uncertainty cannot create a happy outcome. Instead, accept probabilities, possibilities and chance.

8. **It is best to take the easy way out**. Instead of facing the difficulties of life, you may be tempted to try to avoid responsibility or facing the facts. Usually though the 'easy way' turns out to be the harder way. It is better to face the facts head on.

9. **You are not strong enough by yourself.** Many people buy into the belief that they can't survive without someone or something else to depend on for strength. Acting independently may seem riskier at first but leads to greater pay-offs in the long term.

10. **You are a victim of the past**. If something has affected you in the past you do not have to be its permanent victim. Instead, look upon the past as a source of learning and resources.

11. **Happiness should just happen**. The idea that anything happens without effort is again a disempowering 'victim' belief. Focus instead on what you feel happiest doing and do more of it.

More rational beliefs
These are useful beliefs to hold instead.

1. **You can change your feelings and it is useful to do so**. Unwanted feelings do not have to be permanent. It is positive to feel and to be able to express your feelings. It is not useful to be a slave to them.

2. **Your past does not control your future. You can learn from the past and use it as a positive resource for your future.** Just because you have had a particular problem in the past does not mean it

must know

Don't be controlled by emotions
It is important to remember that by understanding the unconscious beliefs and thought patterns we have that produce our emotions we can gain control over them.

has to be a part of your future. Your past and your future are different, even though you may be afraid that this may not be the case. You may feel stuck in or overwhelmed by emotions but people with healthy brains (the majority of us) can have control over their emotions. Your future emotions will only be determined by your new thought patterns.

3. Every person's experiences are unique. Everyone has their own life and own view of life, based on their own experiences, thoughts, beliefs and values. When you 'suffer' negative feelings it may seem that you are the only one to go through what you are experiencing. As a result you may feel alone, different or inadequate in relation to others. It is true that you may be feeling differently from other people – your symptoms may be less or more severe than theirs. It doesn't, however, make you any better or worse than them. Forget about making comparisons; you may never know how others feel because you can't mind read and many people disguise their emotions and put on a public front. It is more useful to focus on examining and challenging your thought patterns and finding a way of creating new feelings for yourself.

4. To create change, willpower is not as useful as changing the meaning you give to events. Thinking and emotional patterns are unconscious habits. If you haven't been able to solve your problems in the past through 'trying hard', CBT may still be able to help you. You can't resolve anything until you have an effective method to do so. If you have picked up unhelpful thinking habits, CBT will provide you with tools to undo them and substitute new, more effective habits.

5. You are an OK person as you are, right now. Because you haven't been able to get rid of certain thoughts and reactions doesn't make you 'broken' or 'bad'. None of us is perfect. We all have our good points and our faults. Make sure you get rid of any unhelpful labels you might be tempted to give yourself. It is important not to beat yourself up because you haven't been able to solve your negative feelings in the past. Remember, you can't be expected to know these methods already. We are not taught at school how to address thinking habits in a rational manner. You are fine as you are AND you now have the opportunity to learn a new skill.

6. **You can't please everyone all of the time**. You can never be certain that anybody will love, like or approve of you. By trying to make them like you, you undermine your identity. It is more important to find out your own interests, look at your personal values and actively cultivate happiness and happy friendships.

7. **It's not what happens to you that is important but how you react to it**. Things you don't like will continue to happen to you. You can't make life perfect or have everything your own way. What you can do is change the way in which the events you experience affect you. Remember, it is not the events themselves but your thoughts about them that are influencing you. Challenge your unhelpful thoughts and determine that if you don't like the way something is affecting you, either to change the situation, minimize its impact or to accept it and move on. Bear in mind that most worries never materialize. The outcomes you desire are most likely to come about by you taking action, not by ruminating about all the awful possibilities.

8. **Facing 'problems' is more useful than avoiding them**. Avoidance doesn't create long-term or permanent change. It may provide a short-term solution or seemingly easy way out but it just postpones the issue. Facing problems will enhance your confidence, give you new skills and lead to long-term change.

9. **You are responsible for your own happiness and you have all the resources inside yourself to create it**. Other people can't 'make you' happy or unhappy. Take responsibility for the life you create. You don't need to be dependent on anyone else

must know

It's OK to live your own life
It's OK to be happy even if other people are not. Give yourself permission to bring neutral and positive feelings into your life. You don't need to share other people's faulty thinking.

to fulfil your life or to create positive feelings. Your thoughts and beliefs can do this for you. If you don't yet know how to create these changes, you can learn.

10. Other people have all the resources they need as well. It is nice to help people and to be empathetic. It is not useful, however, to you or others to 'rescue' them or help them to become dependent on you for their solutions. Each of us is responsible for our own reactions to problems and finding our own solutions. It may be useful to show someone a strategy to solve their problems but not to give them the solution.

11. You are fallible (and being imperfect is good enough). Give up looking for the perfect solution – there may never be one but there may be several useful and workable options. Find out what happens when you just do things to see 'what if'. Perfectionism will bring you anxiety and a sense of failure. Being experimental brings lessons to learn from and positive new thoughts and emotions.

Case study

Lucy is a married woman in her 30s. Fourteen years ago her closest friend and her brother both emigrated within a few months of each other. Although Lucy was married, she had been living a very separate life from her husband for several years. She described the marriage as 'emotionally sterile'. She began to feel frequently depressed and went see her GP for advice. She was recommend-ed a course of six sessions of CBT. In her sessions, she identified her thoughts about herself as, 'I am unlikable'. At the end of each day she highlighted what her feelings had been that day and what had triggered them. She saw her Cognitive Behavioural Therapist on a weekly basis and gradually she began to challenge her negative automatic thoughts.

The first week, Lucy came to the therapy session with a typical example of a trigger situation that led to her feeling depressed. She had seen some people she knew on the other side of the road during the week. They had appeared to ignore her. This reinforced her belief – 'people don't like me'. In the session, she discussed other possible explanations with her therapist. For example, perhaps the people hadn't seen her.

In six sessions, Lucy gradually came to the conclusion 'I am a likable person'. She added, 'If some people don't like me that's just how it is.' Lucy is now divorced, has remarried and is in a very happy relationship.

'Looking back at the CBT now,' she says 'it was amazingly effective. It seems a trite way of turning around negatives to positives but it did work. I have been through worse things over the last few years than in the past and have been unhappy sometimes but I never went back to that same depressed feeling. I always thought – there's a way back from it. It's not about me.'

want to know more?
• To find a therapist to work with, visit The British Association for Behavioural and Cognitive Psychotherapies website, www.babcp.org.uk. They keep a list of accredited individuals in the UK.
• Chapter 4 has more information on setting goals.
• Chapter 5 explains how to change meaning using ABC sheets.

4 Setting goals

This chapter contains instructions for setting yourself achievable goals. What do you want to use CBT for? What problems would you like to overcome? Use the worksheets in this chapter to begin your thinking process and to get clear about what you want to achieve.

Setting goals

It is important that you have well thought-out goals which you really want to achieve because if your goals are not well thought out, you might find that you no longer want them when you finally get them.

must know

Choosing goals

If you lack inspiration, think of things you currently do, think and feel. What would you like less or more of ?

What is a goal?

A goal is simply an end result you want to achieve and can work towards. Goals are most powerful when they are defined as specifically as possible and you are really clear why you want them. Here are some starting principles for setting achievable goals.

Decide what you want to get rid of and what you want more of in your life. Make sure you don't censor your list at all at this stage. Just write down your initial

Example worksheet: what I would like less of/more of

What I want to experience less of/ don't want any more (do, think, feel)	What I want instead/to experience more of (do, think, feel)
• I don't want to feel angry with my ex-boyfriend any more	• I want to feel calm when I see my ex-boyfriend in future
• I don't want to panic when I see spiders	• I want to feel calm when I encounter a spider
• I don't want to think I am a failure	• I want to feel I like myself
• I don't want to think that I am ugly and no one will ever find me attractive again	• I want to think that I am attractive
• I don't want to feel lonely all the time	• I want to be content with how my life is
• I don't want to be fat any more	• I want to slim down
• I don't want to get panic attacks when I go to parties	• I want to feel happy and calm when I go to parties
• I don't want to say 'yes' to things I don't want to do any more	• I want to be able to say 'no' and stick to my decision calmly and assertively

thoughts as they come into your mind. Take as many copies as you need of this sheet and use it to brainstorm what you want to change in your life and what you would like to have instead of your current problems and symptoms.

Worksheet: what I would like less of/more of

What I want to experience less of/ don't want any more (do, think, feel)	What I want instead/to experience more of (do, think, feel)

SMART goals

The SMART goal-setting model is one of the most effective and easy-to-follow methods for creating practical and well-formed achievable goals. SMART goals are clear and precise.

Specific

Be clear and detailed about what you want and where, and with whom you want it. What you want may be a new feeling or a new behaviour. For example, you may want to feel able to take a new career step and feel good about yourself as you do new things.

Measurable

A measurable goal has clear goal posts – points at which you can measure the progress you have made and how far you have to go. A goal post is a piece of concrete evidence that is easy to measure; it allows you to celebrate small successes.

How will you know that you are making progress towards your goal? How often will you check your progress? How will you know when you have reached your goal? What is it going to look like, sound like, feel like to have your new goal? State as clearly as possible the evidence you will be able to observe and that will let you know you have achieved your goal.

Attainable/achievable

Well-formed goals are attainable by you. They depend on you taking the steps to reach them, rather than other people.

must know

SMART GOALS
SMART stands for
1. Specific
2. Measurable
3. Attainable/achievable
4. Realistic
5. Timed

Check your goals
• Are they self-initiated and self-maintained?
• Are they for you and achievable by you?
• Do you want your goal enough to achieve it?
• If not, what would need to change for you to have that amount of commitment?

An attainable goal is also stretching but not so huge that you feel it would be impossible for you to reach.

Realistic
What is the gap between where you are now and your goal? Make a realistic assessment of what it will take to achieve it.

What resources do you already have to help you reach your goal? These may be your internal skills and knowledge or external support from other people.

A skill gap need not permanently stop you from getting your goals. If you don't have the skills currently, you can always acquire them. If a goal is unrealistic at present, is the situation one that you can change?

Timed
The best goals have a time frame – by not having one you are setting yourself up for failure. Putting a date to a goal gives you something to work towards. It also allows you to mark goal posts along the way and helps you to maintain motivation and measure your progress. By doing this you will be able to tweak your goals if necessary to make sure you stay on track to your target. Your overall goal date acts as a deadline which helps to give the goal a sense of importance

must know

Be clear about your goals
• Example of an unclear goal: I want to lose weight.
• Example of a clear goal: I will have lost 3 kilograms in weight by Easter and will weigh 55 kilograms.

and ensures that you stay dedicated and committed to it.

Helpful tips for goals

Here are some tips to help you write effective personal goals.

1. **Brainstorm 'your wants' and 'don't wants'.** Write down what you want to experience as much of as possible and what you want to avoid as much as possible. This will be a mix of feelings, thoughts and/or behaviours.

2. **Change your 'don't wants' into goals.** A goal is what you want to move towards, not away from. For example, 'I don't want arguments with my partner any more,' can be changed to 'I want to communicate effectively with my partner'. Remember to work *towards* goals and not *away from* problems.

3. **Write down what you really want.** And this means everything – be careful not to censor yourself at this stage. It is easy to start thinking 'I won't be able to get that'; 'I shouldn't have this'. Write it all down, whether you think it is possible or probable to have what you want. Remember, as your thoughts and beliefs change, your perspective about what is possible may also change.

4. **Set both short- and long-term goals.** A long-term goal might be to create a new romantic relationship. A short-term goal might be to sit down for five minutes each day and fill in a diary about your activities and emotions.

5. **Set your goals in context.** If you have more than one goal, make sure that they are aligned. If you have a small goal, make sure that it is set in the context of the larger outcome. If you have a short-

term goal, make sure it is aligned with your longer-term ones.

6. Ask yourself how important it is to you to have these goals. Uncover your motivation and commitment to making change. If a goal feels really pressing you are more likely to take consistent action to get it. What will you have more of or less of in your life when you have created this change? Be really clear about what getting your goals will mean to you. If they don't mean much what will keep you taking actions towards them? How motivated are you really going to be? Go back and set some goals you are really passionate about.

7. What are the costs and consequences of your goals?
Who will be affected when you achieve your goals? Are the costs and consequences of getting your goals worth the effort to you? Run a mental film of you achieving your goal through your mind: how do you like what you see, hear and feel yourself having, being and doing? If you don't like everything in your movie change your goals until you feel really comfortable with them.

8. What resources do you have and need to achieve your goals?
What resources do you have available to you now and what extra resources do you need? What support could you ask for and from where?

9. Measure and reward your goals. Your goals are only useful to you if you measure your progress against them. Remember to keep a check on your progress and to reward yourself for each small step you take.

Worksheet: Long-, medium- and short-term goals

must know

Goals
Avoid absolute and perfectionist thinking. Remember your goal list is a 'wish' list, not a 'have to' list. If you don't get a particular goal you can set other goals that will also make you happy. Your goals are simply your preferences for what you would like to happen.

Taking as many copies of the worksheet as you need, write down your goals using the SMART formula on pages 80-1.

First: turn your immediate wants into specific, measurable goals.
Second: look at the list of goals you now have. What other life goals would you like to add?
Tip: think about how you want your life to be. What will it be like when you can say you love your life, you love who you are with, you love what you do, how you are as a person and how you spend your time? Add any goals that you really want to achieve and that will keep you motivated.

Worksheet

SMART Goal	Date

Worksheet

SMART Goal	Date

want to know more?
• For information on well-formed outcomes see *Need to Know? NLP*, Carolyn Boyes, Harper Collins; *5-minute NLP* (Collins Gem), Carolyn Boyes, Collins;
• Re-read the section on faulty thinking in Chapter 2.
• Chapter 3 has advice on making changes in your life.

5 Changing thoughts and feelings

Now it's time to look at practical ways in which you can use CBT to overcome your unwanted thoughts and feelings and to have more positive emotions in your life. By using the worksheets in this chapter you will change the meaning you give to events.

Changing thoughts and feelings

This chapter provides you with a number of worksheets along with advice on how to use them. Photocopy as many worksheets as you need and fill them in, using CBT to combat your own symptoms.

must know

Using the worksheets
You may photocopy the worksheets in this book as many times as you want. Keep referring back to your ABC sheets to see how your thinking develops.

ABC worksheets

The ABC worksheets are the core of your work with CBT. Use them to change the meaning that you give to different situations. By filling them in you will change your inner dialogue to produce a new and healthier reaction to situations. Keep a record of your ABC sheets to see how your feelings change. It is important to identify the underlying beliefs you have about your initial thoughts and what you think about these thoughts.

Example 1: ABC worksheet

A. Activating event you experienced about which you had a negative feeling. *What I was aware of*	B. Irrational belief or irrational evaluation you had about this activating event. *What I thought*	C. Consequences (emotional and behavioural) of your irrational belief. *1. What I felt* *2. What I did*
My boyfriend didn't return my calls for a week.	(First thoughts you are aware of about the situation.) He doesn't love me.	Angry, depressed, worried.

A more complete worksheet would look like this:

Example 2: ABC worksheet

A. Activating event you experienced about which you felt a negative feeling. *What I was aware of*	B. Irrational belief or irrational evaluation you had about this activating event. *What I thought*	C. Consequences (emotional and behavioural) of your irrational belief. *1. What I felt* *2. What I did*
My boyfriend didn't return my calls for a week.	**Initial thought =** He doesn't love me. **Underlying beliefs/ assumptions =** I am not lovable; I don't believe that men are faithful; I am always destined to be alone in life; I have bad relationships; I believe that there is something wrong with me – maybe I am a bad person? **What I think about these thoughts =** I don't like the fact that he didn't return my calls. I don't like the thought that he doesn't love me.	Angry, depressed, worried

You can complete your own ABC worksheet on the next page.

5 Changing thoughts and feelings

Worksheet 1: ABC worksheet

A. Activating event you experienced about which you felt a negative feeling. *What I was aware of.* (e.g. Someone said something to me I didn't like hearing).	B. Irrational belief or irrational evaluation you had about this activating event. *What I thought* (e.g. I must be liked by everyone).	Thinking error: Identify the thinking error behind these thoughts (e.g. 'must', 'should', 'ought', all-or-nothing thinking).	C. Consequences (emotional and behavioural) of your irrational belief. *1. What I felt.* *2. What I did.* (e.g. felt upset, over-ate and drank too much).

1. Observe and capture your thoughts and beliefs Capture/analyse your beliefs and thoughts about a particular problem, situation or event. The way to do this is to pay attention to your feelings: when you notice any negative changes in your emotions, observe the thoughts that have come into your mind. Write these down. This will allow you to look at them at a later point and analyse them.

must know

Tip
Use the advice in Chapter 2 – Faulty thinking – to uncover your unhelpful thinking habits.

2. What beliefs do these thoughts imply? What do you believe about yourself, other people and the world at large in relation to the trigger event?

3. Check the context of your current beliefs. What is true in one context may not be true in another. Beliefs are formed over many years and as a result of the amalgamation of your experiences. You may have a very different understanding of the world now from that when you first formed your beliefs but you have not yet addressed the discrepancy between your beliefs and your current evidence. Or what may be true in one context may not be true in another.

Examples of checking the context of current beliefs:

• *I am a failure in relationships because I am not married at 27 years old.*
This belief has formed because the speaker is surrounded by a peer group who are all married. By alerting himself to this belief, he becomes aware that in other situations there are groups containing

people older than him who are not married. He begins to challenge this belief.

must know

Be careful
Remember, the more accurate and rational you can get with your thoughts, the more you will eliminate faulty thinking patterns and negative emotions.

• *I am stupid*
This belief has formed because the speaker failed his exams at school. He is now a successful manager yet the belief has remained an unconscious obstacle which influences his expectations of further promotions at work and general interactions with colleagues.

Doing a Camera Check

If you are not sure whether your current thinking is useful to you or not, consider using this technique. It is based on what M.C. Maultsby, a rational emotive therapist, calls the Camera Check of Perception.

Imagine that you had a camera and could film your current situation. What would you see when you played the tape back?

A film shows only the facts, not our perception. It does not show all the distortions and deletions of facts or how we have amplified or minimized certain pieces of the picture to produce a perspective on it. A picture captures the events starkly.

For example, you think: 'She says she is going to be home on time in the evenings. But she is never home on time,' (generalization).

Camera Check challenge:
If you were to take a picture of the situation what would it show? Is she ever home on time?
You: 'Well, a camera would show that she has been late three times this week.'

The difference shows up the irrational thought pattern for what it is. This kind of check is a useful metaphor you can use as a tool to get your facts straight and to identify faulty thinking.

ABCDEF worksheet

The next stage is to challenge these thoughts. You can now add DEF to your ABCs. The worksheet on pages 94–5 allows you to note down your existing ABCs, to question their validity and to come up with alternative thoughts.

Result: new constructive actions
So, continuing with the scenario in the worksheet on page 89, the next time you see him, you explain how you feel about phone calls as indicators of how he feels. You become more accepting of his fallibility.

Working with worksheets

Take your time over each sheet you fill in. Remember, practise will make all the difference, allowing your new thoughts to replace old, automatic ones.

Example of an ABCDEF worksheet

A. Activating event you experienced about which you had a negative feeling *What I was aware of* (e.g. Someone said something to me I didn't like hearing).	B. Irrational belief or irrational evaluation you had about this activating event. *What I thought* (e.g. I must be liked by everyone).	C. Consequences (emotional and behavioural) of your irrational belief. *1. What I felt* *2. What I did* (e.g. Feeling upset and over-eating and drinking).
Your boyfriend is away and has forgotten to call you even though you had arranged the call in advance. This situation has triggered upset and anger.	He doesn't love me, that's why he hasn't called; I am not lovable; he should see things my way; he should know that not calling will upset me; he has to call me; I don't know what to do if he doesn't call me; I feel like a relationship failure.	You feel upset, hurt and angry. When he eventually calls you end up having a big argument and feel even worse about yourself and your relationship.

D. Disputing or questioning your irrational belief (e.g. Why must I be liked by everyone?).	E. Effective new thinking or answer/the result of challenging your original irrational belief (e.g. Although I prefer people don't say things to me I don't want to hear, there is nothing to say that they 'must not').	F. New feelings and actions that resulted from disputing your irrational belief (e.g. calmness, eating and drinking normally).
Why must he see things my way? Why does not calling have to mean that he doesn't love me?	Perhaps he is busy at work and so has so much going on he couldn't face calling anyone; perhaps he doesn't realize how important it is to me to have a call; perhaps he doesn't relate how often he calls to whether he loves me; I don't like people breaking their promises to me but I do understand that he is an imperfect human being; I will let him know that when he does or does not keep his promise to do something it has a connection with how I feel that he feels about me; when he doesn't call I feel hurt.	Irritated but not angry.

ABCDEF Worksheet (Take as many copies as you need.

A. Activating event you experienced about which you had a negative feeling *What I was aware of* (e.g. Someone said something to me I didn't like hearing).	B. Irrational belief or irrational evaluation you had about this activating event. *What I thought* (e.g. I must be liked by everyone).	C. Consequences (emotional and behavioural) of your irrational belief. 1. *What I felt* 2. *What I did* (e.g. Feeling upset and over-eating and drinking).

Use these worksheets to keep a record of your change in thinking.)

D. Disputing or questioning your irrational belief (e.g. Why must I be liked by everyone?).	E. Effective new thinking or answer/the result of challenging your original irrational belief (e.g. Although I prefer people don't say things to me I don't want to hear, there is nothing to say that they 'must not').	F. New feelings and actions that resulted from disputing your irrational belief (e.g. calmness, eating and drinking normally).

Increase your emotional vocabulary

If you want to gain more control over your feelings it is useful to increase your vocabulary when naming them. This stops any tendency to overgeneralize. Use the list below to be more specific

Feelings checklist

These words can be used to describe your state of mind. What feeling are you really experiencing when you have an unpleasant emotion?

Aggressive	Cut-up	Free	Livid	Shocked
Aggrieved	Degraded	Fuming	Lonely	Shy
Agitated	Deplorable	Furious	Malevolent	Small
Angry	Depressed	Futile	Malicious	Sour
Annoyed	Diminished	Grief-stricken	Marred	Spiteful
Anxious	Dirty	Grumpy	Melancholic	Strong
Apprehensive	Disbelieving	Guilty	Moody	Sullied
Ashamed	Discouraged	Gutted	Mortified	Tearful
Awkward	Disenchanted	Harmed	Mournful	Tense
Bad-tempered	Disillusioned	Heart-sick	Nervous	Thwarted
Belittled	Displeased	Hideous	Offended	Timid
Bereft	Distraught	Horrible	Outraged	Touchy
Bitter	Distressed	Humiliated	Pain (in)	Troubled
Blameworthy	Docile	Hurt	Pained	Truculent
Blue	Dogmatic	Ignorant	Paranoid	Unconfident
Bothered	Doubtful	Ill-tempered	Peevish	Uneasy
Calm	Downcast	Incapacitated	Perplexed	Unforgivable
Chaotic	Downhearted	Inconsolable	Prickly	Unpardonable
Comatose	Edgy	Insecure	Relieved	Unsure
Concerned	Enraged	Inspired	Resentful	Vexed
Confident	Envious	Irritated	Restless	Wary
Confounded	Fearful	Jealous	Self-conscious	Worried
Crestfallen	Forgiving	Jumpy	Self-doubt	Wounded
Cross	Fractious	Let down	Shattered	Wronged

about the feelings you experience in response to trigger situations so that you can be very clear when these feelings change.

Belief rating

Keep clear on the progress you are making towards your goals by checking your belief and commitment to your new thoughts and feelings.

On your record sheet, keep a check on how your belief in your thoughts is changing. To do this, it is useful to rate how strongly you believe a particular thought with 0 equalling 'no belief' and 10 equalling 'I totally believe this thought'.

Rate both your belief in the first irrational thoughts accompanying the anxiety and then, after you have come up

Example - Belief rating record:

A Activating event you experienced about which you had a negative feeling. *What I was aware of*	B. Irrational belief or irrational evaluation you had about this activating event. *What I thought*	Rate belief in automatic thoughts (0-10)	E. Effective new thinking or answer – the result of challenging your original irrational belief.	Re-rate belief in negative automatic thoughts (0-10).	Finally, rate belief in effective new thinking 0-10.
Your boyfriend has forgotten to call you.	He doesn't love me.	8	Perhaps he is busy at work and has so much going on he couldn't face calling anyone.	5	8

Belief rating record (Take as many copies as you need)

A Activating event you experienced about which you had a negative feeling. *What I was aware of*	B. Irrational belief or irrational evaluation you had about this activating event. *What I thought*	Rate belief in automatic thoughts (0-10)	E. Effective new thinking or answer – the result of challenging your original irrational belief.	Re-rate belief in negative automatic thoughts (0-10).	Finally, rate belief in effective new thinking 0-10.

with a more rational response, look back at the original thoughts and re-rate your response to them. Finally, rate your level of belief in the new rational thoughts.

Mood diary

You may find it useful to use a mood diary. Record how your mood changes as you use the ABC sheets over several weeks. Each day, estimate how you have been feeling on a scale of 0– 100 per cent.

want to know more?
• *What You Can Change and What You Can´t: The Complete Guide to Successful Self-Improvement* by Martin E. P. Seligman.
• **For advice on setting goals, see Chapter 4.**
• **Chapter 6 has tips on overcoming resistance to change.**

Example - Mood Diary

	Week 1	Week 2	Week 3	Week 4	Week 5
Monday	50%	50%	40%	30%	0%
Tuesday	70%	50%	40%	20%	10%
Wednesday	70%	50%	30%	0%	0%
Thursday	60%	60%	30%	10%	0%
Friday	50%	40%	50%	0%	20%
Saturday	80%	60%	30%	10%	0%
Sunday	80%	60%	40%	30%	10%

Mood Diary (Take as many copies as you need)

	Week 1	Week 2	Week 3	Week 4	Week 5
Monday					
Tuesday					
Wednesday					
Thursday					
Friday					
Saturday					
Sunday					

6 Overcoming resistance to change

Sometimes as you work towards change you can meet a block. This chapter looks at some of the reasons why you may be resistant to change and what you can do to alter this.

Overcoming resistance to change

Resistance to therapy or to change in general can surface on occasions. These are some of the reasons why this happens and how you can overcome them.

must know

Some reasons why people are afraid of change
1. Secondary gain e.g. loss of attention: I might lose the power of being a victim, a relationship, the way of life I have.
2. Shame and Punishment: 'I/they don't deserve to change.'
3. Unrealistic expectations of change.
4. Not recognizing success.
5. Pessimism: things might get worse, not better.

Secondary gain

Secondary gain is the (often unconscious) benefit someone gets from having a problem, even though it appears to be beneficial for them to get rid of it.

Some unconscious beliefs behind secondary gain:

• *'Without this problem I won't get this benefit. Therefore it is a bad idea for me to get rid of this problem.'*
• *'This is the only way to get this benefit.'*
• *'I am right to feel like this, I am only human.'*
• *'This is the fastest/easiest way to get this benefit.'*

For example, a man who often feels depressed may not enjoy the emotional distress the depression brings but he has a secondary gain of receiving attention from his children.

A woman feels lonely and anxious. Her husband and friends give her love and affection when she is in this state. She is afraid if she starts to feel good about herself and gets rid of the worry, she will lose these positive feelings from her friends and family.

How to overcome secondary gain

Using the general tools of CBT may uncover some of the unhelpful beliefs a person has, causing him to assume that he needs this secondary gain. Here are some additional questions you can ask yourself:

- *'Is thinking, feeling, or doing things this way the best route I can take (not just the easiest)?'*
- *'Is it in my best interests to carry on feeling, or doing things this way?'*
- *'What else could I do, think or feel to get me the goals I want and help me to feel the way I want to feel?'*

Shame and punishment

Another reason why some people are resistant to therapy is because they feel they should punish themselves or because they are afraid of revealing something 'shameful' they have done in the past.

Shame

Sometimes the reason a person creates bad thought and emotion cycles is because of the beliefs attached to an event in the past. They may have done something or thought something about which they are ashamed. This person then faces a dilemma, because they want help to resolve this situation but are ashamed of revealing what a 'bad person' they are.

What may happen is that the person gives clues or hints about the problem to their therapist but won't disclose the whole set of beliefs; they may not even be totally aware of it themselves because it has been so well buried in the unconscious.

Punishment

Sometimes a person is willing to 'tell all' but is resistant to change because they feel that they are deserving of the punishment of negative feelings.

A typical belief is 'I have done bad things/thought bad thoughts and so I don't deserve to be happy.' This type of belief may come from what we have been told by authority figures as children or sometimes what we are told by religion.

How to overcome feelings of shame
If you find that your resistance is in explaining your current feelings to a therapist, remember:
• A therapist is not a mind reader.
• The judgement is in your mind.
• The therapist's role is to help you. You need not seek their approval.

How to overcome feelings of 'needing punishment'
If you experience the sorts of thoughts outlined above, remember:
• A person is not the same as his or her behaviour. If you have done something you are not proud of, you are more than that one behaviour.
• Check the cause and effect link: were you really responsible for the negative outcome of the event?
• Check your beliefs around punishment: who says you have to suffer as a consequence of what happened? What would happen if you decided to adopt a different belief?

Unrealistic expectations of change
A third reason for resistance to change is unrealistic expecta-tions. Often change builds gradually. We make a small change and then another. Before long our thoughts and emotions are different without us having realized. Several beliefs can undermine this.

Instant change
The first belief is a 'need' for instant change. Of course it would be wonderful if change happened straight away. Indeed, with

CBT you may experience some comparatively quick results as it uses fewer sessions than conventional talking therapies, some of which continue for years.

However, don't put yourself under pressure to achieve instant results. Of course you want relief from the negative feelings you have experienced, especially if they have been ongoing over several years, but remember if you stick with CBT and use its tools consistently, you are likely to see real changes that stick.

Failure or feedback?

The second block is a belief in failure. If you believe in failure, you will expect instant success or give up. If you believe in 'feedback' you will look at everything you do as a step on in your change.

If you don't see results straight away, ask yourself:

• *What have I given up in the past because I thought I had failed?*
• *What new approaches could solve the problem?*
• *What would happen if I stuck with this for a bit longer?*

Remember: if you apply the tools you have and work towards the goals you want you *will* create change. Thomas Edison is said to have *failed* to make a lightbulb that worked 1,000 times before succeeding.

Successes develop directly out of failures. By seeing each failure as feedback about what you can do differently next time, you will learn to develop a success habit. Failure is a great personal coach. Whatever you do, keep on going. Most people give up when right around the corner what they really want is waiting for them.

Not recognizing success

It is important to be really clear what success will look, sound and feel like when you get it. If you have experienced negative feelings such as depression or anxiety you are no doubt only too

Failure
'Many of life's failures
are people who did not
realize how close they
were to success when
they gave up.' *Thomas
Alva Edison*

'Never confuse a single
defeat with a final
defeat.' *F. Scott
Fitzgerald*

Making permanent
changes always involves
a belief in feedback as
opposed to failure. This
gives you an attitude of
tenacity, motivation and
the assumption that you
have the ability to
achieve a positive
outcome.

aware of what these feel like. But what will it be like
when these are gone?

Many people have a false expectation that these
unpleasant feelings will be replaced with equally
strong positive feelings such as extreme happiness.
It is very important to recognize that the opposite of
negative feelings is calmness, not wild exhilaration.

All these issues can be challenged. Identify and
work through your beliefs. Observe what thoughts
and emotions are currently habits in your life using
the CBT worksheets.

Pessimism and negative thoughts about change

Negative thoughts can stop you from taking or
continuing to take action which interrupts your
vicious cycles.

On pages 109–10 you will find some common
thoughts and challenges to them.

Challenging blocks with a costs/ benefits analysis

In any situation where you want to make a choice
about your thinking it is useful to do a costs/benefits
analysis.

Think about the change you want to achieve.
Check back to the goals you have set yourself. What
is your commitment to them? The exercise on page
111 gives you a structure to explore and overcome
your resistance to change.

Common objections	Challenges
There's no point starting/carrying on – I won't succeed.	I don't know what will happen until I take action. If I do something different it is highly likely I will get a different result. If I don't get the result I want it doesn't matter. It is OK to learn and move on to another action.
It's too late to do anything now.	The past does not determine the future. It might have been a good idea if I had done something in the past but that has gone now. It is better to let go of any guilt about it, stop beating myself up and do something now.
This looks like hard work. I am not good at doing practical things like keeping diaries, filling in sheets or keeping schedules.	What would I be doing to take practical steps if I wasn't feeing negative? I have done difficult things before. Who could I ask to help and support me to take the steps I would like to take? I can start by taking little steps – just making some notes in the book or on a piece of paper would be a positive step.
I feel overwhelmed by it all. I should start when I am feeling more positive.	I may be feeling overwhelmed because I feel anxious and depressed. If I start writing down how I feel I can get a grip on what can be done and I might start to feel more positive.
I won't like doing this.	I won't know how I feel about doing it until I start doing it. I can't see the future.
I don't know how to do all the things I am supposed to do to change.	It is fine just to experiment and see what happens – not to be perfect in everything I do.
I don't know what to do as a starting point.	Anything I do will have a result. Once I take one positive step it becomes easier to take the next.
I just don't want to do this.	Maybe that's true. So what are the costs to me of not taking steps? What are the benefits to me of taking steps?

Common objections:	Challenges
I haven't managed to achieve much so far. I might as well give up.	For some people, what I have achieved might not look much. But for me, keeping a list, going for a walk, filling in my ABC sheet are achievements. I deserve to congratulate myself on every achievement in recognition of the real progress I have made.
If I fail I will feel worse than I do now and I already feel a failure.	I won't know how I will really feel until I do something. By taking action I may change my thoughts about being a failure. It's human to be fallible. I may find the evidence to support that belief by taking action and 'acting as if'.
I am afraid of what will happen if I am successful. Maybe I won't like the life I have.	What benefits do I get from the life I have now? What are the costs? What benefits could I get with change in my life? Perhaps it is time to look at the fears I have about change and face them.

want to know more?

• Also see Overcoming Blocks in *Need to Know? NLP* by Carolyn Boyes, HarperCollins.
• Read Chapter 2 for an analysis of different types of faulty thinking.

If you want to change your beliefs and emotions, be careful with the language you use to describe yourself. The idea that you 'suffer from' a particular condition endows it with the idea of permanence or illness. It may be more useful to think that you are 'anxious' – a temporarily occurring feeling and behaviour that can be combated – rather than 'suffering from anxiety' – a more permanent sounding condition.

Think carefully about your attitudes and beliefs, feelings and behaviours and how your life will be if you do or don't change them. Weigh up the benefits and the costs to you of changing and not changing and decide what you want to do.

A- Activating situation	Benefits	How strongly do you feel about this?	Costs	How strongly do you feel about this?
Describe the nature of the event that triggers unpleasant consequences for you.	*What are the benefits of not changing the way you think, act and feel?*	*Rate the importance you give to each factor*	*What are the costs of not changing?*	*Rate the importance you give to each factor*
	For you		For you	
	For the world		For the world	
	For your friends and family		For your friends and family	
	Immediately		Immediately	
	In the medium term		In the medium term	
	In the long term		In the long term	

7 Anger

Anger is a very normal response to perceived pain, hurt and injustice. The word 'perceived' is important because anger is a direct result of the way you view the world. In this chapter, we explore anger, why it is harmful, and how to overcome it using CBT.

Anger

Anger is not caused by other people. It is, like other emotions, an automatic response to how you perceive an event that you have classified as a distressful situation.

must know

Causes of anger
Nobody 'makes' you angry. You 'make yourself' angry.

Anger and health

Have you ever caught yourself saying something like:

- *'He made me really angry.'*
- *'Every time she says that it drives me mad.'*
- *'I was having a great day and then that driver cut in and made me furious. He ruined my day.'*

All of the above are misconceptions.

There are two schools of thought on anger. One believes that there is a difference between healthy (appropriate) and unhealthy (inappropriate) anger. This school holds that it is sometimes appropriate to express (let out) your anger and that suppressing (or not expressing) it is unhealthy.

The other school of thought, supported by recent research, believes that all anger is harmful and unhealthy and it makes no difference whether you express or suppress it. According to this way of thinking, expressing anger can cause negative physiological effects. Links have been found between arthritis and anger. It has also been suggested in several research projects that hostile, competitive 'type A' personalities are more likely to suffer heart problems than others. Conversely, people who suppress their anger when they have been hurt can set up depressive thinking.

What other options are there? A third way of thinking about anger is to not feel it in the first place. The way to do this is to learn a new way of thinking about the situations you encounter.

Faulty thinking behind anger

'Musts', 'shoulds' and 'oughts' and rigid beliefs and demands underlie anger:

• Thinking that the other person should obey our rigid rules is a sure way to create anger.
• All-or-nothing thinking: assuming that you are right and other people are wrong.
• Seeing only one perspective: thinking that there is only one way to view an event.
• Believing that the world should be fair and just.
• Believing that people should not disagree with you or disrespect you.
• Believing that you 'should' be perfect and it's not OK to have weaknesses; so if someone criticizes you, you become defensive.
• Believing that you should have what you want whenever you want it in the way that you want it.

Examples of thinking that causes anger

• *He should do what I tell him to.*
• *She should give me presents if she loves me.*
• *He should not be late.*
• *He should be more polite to me when he serves me in the shop.*
• *She should apologize when she is wrong.*
• *She should not tell me what to do now I am an adult.*

must know

Negative effects of anger
• Ongoing thoughts of revenge
• Passive-aggressive behaviour
• Wanting to turn other people against the person you think has hurt you
• Stress and muscle tension
• Fear of being attacked in future – being constantly on alert
• Heart disease: increased likelihood of heart attack, hypertension and stroke
• Increased likelihood of violence and abusive behaviour
• Taking out anger on objects or animals
• Alienating relationships through angry, adversarial attitudes

must know

3 steps to defeat anger
1. Recognize that it is you who are making yourself angry, not the external circumstances.
2. Identify the belief or personal rule you have that is making you angry.
3. Use the ABC method to challenge your faulty thinking.

Defeating anger

The way to defeat anger is first of all to recognize that it is *your* thinking that is making you angry, not the event or the other person.

What about the idea that you have a right to get angry if you are dealing with someone who is being unpleasant or difficult? Well, we can claim any rights we want. The real question is – do we get the results we want by this method?

There are many advantages to not getting angry. Anger reduces effectiveness. When you show anger towards another person it may have the effect of getting them to do what you want but it is very unlikely to create real, permanent behaviour change in the other person. In fact, it is far more likely that if you get angry with someone they will become unpleasant in return. However, if you stay calm or react lovingly to the other person they may modify or change their behaviour.

ABCDEF example for anger

A = Activating event/situation
You have prepared dinner for two friends. One friend arrives on time but your other friend is half an hour late and you have to wait.

B = Beliefs
Your immediate reaction is, 'Why is he always so late? Couldn't he be on time knowing it was important to me? He should be considerate to me and my other friends and he shouldn't be late.'

C = Consequences: feelings and actions

You feel angry. Later that evening you dig at your friend for being late with veiled comments. You sulk through dinner and it is clear to your friends that you are in a bad mood.

D = Dispute

'Why must he be considerate to me and my other friends? Why must he be on time?' You start to question your demands and personal rules about time and treatment.

E = Effective new thinking

'I know he is busy at work at the moment. There is no cosmically ordained rule that says he should treat me in a particular way. I would prefer that he is on time when we make an arrangement or that he calls me and lets me know that he will be late. However, I recognize that he is a fallible human being just like me. Perhaps the most useful thing to do would be to plan for the reality that he is often late. I don't like this fact but there are many good things in our friendship which compensate for this. It's not as if he did it on purpose.'

You decide that in the future you will plan appointments differently to take account of your friend's time-keeping.

F = New feeling

You still feel some upset but this is more at the level of frustration rather than anger or rage.

ABCDEF example 2

A = Activating event/situation

Your husband is away and has forgotten to call you even though you had arranged the call in advance. This situation has triggered upset and anger.

B = Beliefs/automatic thoughts/assumptions
'He doesn't love me that's why he hasn't called.' 'I am not lovable'. 'He should see things my way.' 'He should know that not calling will upset me.' 'He has to call me; I don't know what to do if he doesn't call me. I feel like a relationship failure.'

C = Consequences: feelings and actions
You feel upset, hurt and angry. When he eventually calls you end up having a big argument and feel even worse about yourself and your relationships.

D = Dispute the irrational beliefs
Why must he see things my way? Why does not calling have to mean that he doesn't love me?

E = Effective new thinking
'Perhaps he is busy at work and so has so much going on he couldn't face calling anyone. Perhaps he doesn't realize how important it is to me to have a call. Perhaps he doesn't relate how often he calls to whether he loves me. I don't like people breaking their promises to me but I do understand that he is an imperfect human being.'
  'I will let him know that when he does or does not keep his promise to do something it has a connection with how I feel that he feels about me. When he doesn't call I feel hurt.'

What is the alternative to anger?

There are several options. The first is simply to remain calm. The second is to be assertive. Some people will turn the other cheek when they are confronted with anger.

Assertiveness – an alternative to anger

Assertiveness is the ability to express your opinions, feelings, wants and needs using direct, honest communication without stepping on the rights of other people.

Assertive people
• express what they want
• ask for it clearly
• are not afraid of taking a risk
• express positive and negative feelings
• can refuse requests and invitations
• give and receive compliments
• are calm
• receive and give feedback.

They do not
• get angry and aggressive
• bully
• manipulate

must know

Assertiveness
When you are assertive you express your opinion directly and calmly *without* anger.

• go behind other people's backs

• suppress their angry feelings.

Why be assertive?

1. It is a useful way to avoid creating anger. By learning to take responsibility for your own behaviour and to state your wants and opinions you are reducing the likelihood of getting angry and making it more likely that others will listen to your point of view.

2. It is good for your relationships. If, as often happens in relationships, there is a difference between your point of view and the other person's, you increase the possibility of a win-win situation where both of your needs are met without conflict. Assertiveness increases the probability that you will have honest relationships where you have the respect of other people.

3. Being assertive will enable you to handle different situations which will feed your self-confidence and self-regard. This has a positive spiralling effect, leading to positive automatic thoughts, beliefs and feelings and more assertive behaviour.

4. Assertiveness saves energy that can be used instead to get the goals you want. When you get angry, you use up a lot of energy, stewing about situations or dealing with the consequences of expressing your negative feelings. When you express your wants and needs in a non-aggressive manner,

Beliefs that trigger aggressive behaviour	Beliefs that trigger passive behaviour	Beliefs that trigger assertive behaviour
• I know best. • Other people are wrong and I am right. • They are all useless. • If I attack first I won't get attacked. • Other people aren't trustworthy. • I can't let them get away with saying that. • Others have no right to disagree with me. • My needs are more important than other people's. • I'm more vulnerable if I am seen to be wrong. • It will show weakness if I change my mind.	• They probably are right and I am wrong. I'm usually wrong. • I have no right to ask somebody for something. • If people refuse it means they are rejecting me and don't like me. • My needs are not that important/as important as other people's. • I have to do this 100 per cent right if I am going to do it at all. • My opinion doesn't/I don't really count. • They won't like it if I say what I think or what I want. • It is better not to stir up trouble. • Other people should come first. • Disagreeing leads to unpleasant conflict. • People will think I am being difficult if I disagree. • I might be wrong and then I will look silly. • I don't have the right to disagree.	• Assertiveness is effective. • I am responsible for the results I get in life. • I and others have the right to hold and communicate opinions that may be different. • An opinion is not the same as a fact. • Disagreements do not have to lead to conflict. • I can be positive, empathetic and sensitive in the way I put forward my views. • I am responsible for the effects of my communication. • I can choose how to express myself and how to behave. • I can learn and change.

Some useful beliefs about rights

You have:
• The right to have your own opinion and make decisions without having to justify or explain them to other people.
• The right to ask for what you want and to pursue your own goals.
• The right to lead your own life.
• The right to say 'yes' and the right to say 'no'.
• The right not to understand and to say 'I do not understand'.
• The right to refuse the demands of other people.
• The right not to get involved in other people's problems unless you want to.
• The right to make mistakes.
• The right to privacy.
• The right to change your mind.
• The right to tell others how you wish to be treated.
• The right to change or develop your life.
• The right to like yourself even though you are not perfect.

you will reduce stress and frustration, and be less afraid of other people's reactions.

Rights and responsibilities

Assertiveness involves holding certain beliefs about your rights and responsibilities and the rights you give to other people.

With rights go responsibilities. It is your responsibility to accept that other people have the same rights as you have. They have the right to express their opinions and also to make mistakes.

However, do remember that it is important to balance other people's rights and your own. People who are passive rather than assertive do accept these rights for other people and are ready to forgive their mistakes but may be less sure about these rights or beliefs as they apply to themselves. Passive behaviour is self-denying and can be manipulative.

When you allow the needs and opinions of other people to dominate you are likely to feel angry or hurt whether you show it or suppress it. If you adopt assertive beliefs it will give you an alternative route which will create more positive feelings.

If your tendency is to take a stand for your rights too readily, take care that you are recognizing the rights of others or you will fuel counterproductive aggression and repercussions in relationships.

Communicating assertively

Anger can be avoided by learning to communicate assertively, which will prevent point scoring, bottling up emotions and open arguments.

Communicating with anger highlights disagreement and usually ends in a lose-lose situation where both parties take up polarized positions. Communicating from a passive position means that conflicts of interest and real points of disagreement are not discussed. If these are stored up for discussion later it can trigger conflict after the event.

Communicating from an assertive state means that you can be straight and honest, you don't over-apologize or justify and you don't take refusals personally. You recognize that the other person has the right to refuse a request.

must know

The three components of assertive communication
1. Facts
2. Emotions
3. Needs

Assertive communication relies on a very simple, easy-to-remember formula. You tell the other person, as simply and directly as possible:
1. How you feel (emotion)
2. About what (fact)
3. Why you feel like that (need)
4. At the end of the statement you stop and allow space for your words to be heard. Leaving a space after you have said what you feel is very important as it gives weight to what you are saying.

'I'm very upset
that you didn't call me,
as I put aside time for the call as we agreed.'

'I'm really happy
that you have told me what the issue is
as it helps me to think about a solution.'

Other ways to communicate effectively
Stating your opinion
'In my opinion...'
'As I see it...'

'I find that...'
'I think...'
'I now think'

Stating disagreement
'I see it differently in that...'

Give a reason for your disagreement and state clearly what you disagree with and what you agree with. This avoids the sense that you are simply knocking down the other person's ideas.

Follow a doubt with a suggestion.

Demonstrating understanding
You listen to the other person and demonstrate that you are listening by saying:

'I can see you feel A (emotion)
About B (fact)
When you want C' (need)

Putting forward suggestions
'How about...'
'Shall we...'

Asking for more information
'Have I got this right, you want to...?'

Asking for other peoples' views for a win-win
'What's your opinion?'
'What's your view on...?'

Forgiveness – accepting yourself and others

Forgiveness is an essential tool to use in both self-acceptance and letting go of anger. Forgiving yourself and others allows you to move on from a place of stuckness and negative self-rating to flexibility in thinking.

Forgiveness is defined as the process of letting go and ceasing to feel anger, bitterness or resentment to others or oneself for perceived harm, mistakes or offences and no longer wanting self-punishment or punishment or restitution from others. If, when you read this, you feel uneasy or think of people you would like to 'get back' at, lash out at, or show anger towards, you have forgiveness to do. If you think about your own 'failures', 'lacks' or 'mistakes' you have labels and self-rating to let go of and to forgive.

Forgiving others

It may seem strange to say that forgiving others is part of self-acceptance but in forgiving other people you forgive your part in the situation and reinforce the beliefs that all of us are fallible – including you. Forgiveness has been shown to have both spiritual and physical rewards for the forgiver. It allows you to shrug your shoulders when something you don't like happens and to move on.

Human beings often do things that upset others. Forgiveness doesn't mean having to forget, but we can't move on in our lives unless we forgive.

Forgiving yourself

To achieve self-acceptance, look over your own past and what you classify as your *mistakes*. Forgive

watch out

Forgiveness and health
Clinical studies show that people who forgive are healthier and happier with themselves than people who harbour grievances and resentments. Holding on to non-forgiveness triggers anger and stress, causing release of the stress hormone cortisol. This has been linked with depression, memory deterioration, heart problems and fatigue, as well as wear and tear on the body, showing up in the face and skin. See page 126 for more negative effects.

yourself for them. Look at what you believe other people have done to you in the past. Forgive them. Continuing to hold on to blame and old grievances stops you – not them – from moving on.

Forgiveness and health

Not forgiving has proven effects on health and on how your body functions. When you feel that you have been hurt, betrayed, humiliated or suffered a loss, your body responds with tension and stress. Here are some of the possible effects:

• Blood flow to the heart and skin surfaces is restricted.
• Digestion is negatively affected.
• Your muscles become tighter and may cause pain in your back or neck.
• You may clench your jaw or grind your teeth.
• Diminished blood flow means that the supply of oxygen and nutrients to the cells is reduced.
• You may get more headaches.
• Your immune system is lowered, making you more vulnerable to illness and infection.
• Breathing becomes shallower and restricted.

First examine the beliefs you have that hold the lack of acceptance of the situation as it is in place.

Beliefs that stop forgiveness of others

1. The world is fair and just: when we think that the world should be fair and just we try to make others respond to this belief. When they don't act fairly or justly, we just try harder. Why? Because we believe that

2. Bad things 'should not happen to us'

3. We are morally superior to the person who has done something to us. Feeling that we are in the right justifies us in feeling anger but also stops us making the choice to forgive. If people around us support our story then we gain a secondary benefit from keeping a lack of forgiveness.

Beliefs that stop forgiveness of ourselves

1. I am bad and deserve punishment.
2. Bad things always happen to me.

Non-forgiveness and emotion

• Not forgiving other people leads to anger. If you believe justice should be done and it hasn't been done, it will lead to you feeling anger towards the person you feel has harmed you.
• Not forgiving oneself leads to guilt. If you feel that you have made mistakes or have inadequacies or flaws then you will feel guilt for failing to meet your own high standards.

Rational beliefs that allow forgiveness of self and others

1. **You live in the present not the past.** First of all realize that you cannot change the past. Much as you would like to go back and wipe out what you or another person did, it is done. It seems very obvious to say this, but why we don't forgive is because our minds linger on past hurts, mistakes and injustices. The language that goes with this way of thinking is 'should have' language, for example, *I/he/she should have done this*. Or *I/he/she should not have done this*.
2. **All sorts of things happen to us.** As you know, at the core of CBT thinking is – it is not what happens to us that is important. It is the meaning we give to the events.
3. **You have a choice about what you think, feel and do now.** Change is up to you. If you want self-acceptance, changing your way of thinking about yourself and others is a necessity. We can't make others behave in the way we would like them to. The only thing we can change is how we react to the situation.

ABCs of forgiveness

Take a look at how non-forgiveness affects you using the ABC model.

A – Activating situation	B - Beliefs	C- Consequences
What happened? Think about a situation where you felt another person did you a wrong. Describe the nature of the event.	What are your automatic thoughts about this situation?	What are the emotional, physiological and behavioural consequences for you?
My girlfriend cheated on me.	• It was a terrible thing to do. • She is a horrible, nasty person. • It wasn't fair. I always treated her well. • I loved her. I will never meet anyone like her again. My life is over.	I feel full of grief, depressed and I am very angry at her and carry that anger into other relationships.

Costs/ benefit analysis

In any situation where you want to make a choice about your thinking it is useful to do a costs/benefits analysis (see Chapter 5). When you fill out the form on page 130, think about how you see the situation currently. This is not an easy exercise but it will pay off in real benefits in how you see yourself. It allows you to have a structure to explore your feelings and to look objectively at situations. It will clarify your automatic thoughts and put some distance between you and any uncomfortable emotions you have about situations.

Be honest in your answers. It is highly likely that your thoughts are mixed and inconsistent.

Look at the benefits of not forgiving first of all. These commonly include feelings such as moral superiority to the person who has done the wrong, of being justified in feeling anger, blame or hurt and of feeling rights to retribution or recompense. Rate how important it is to you to continue to feel these things.

Next look at the costs. The emotional costs of not forgiving may be very high. Think about the level of distress you feel. How much anger or anxiety do you have? How much time are you spending thinking (obsessing) about the situation? What effect is it having on your other relationships? How are others reacting to you? What other effects are there on you?

The role of empathy

When you are empathetic, you step into the other person's shoes in your mind in order to positively gain a new perspective on a situation. This helps you to come to a realization of how the situation might have seemed at the time, or seems now, to the other person involved in it.

Remember we all make mistakes. We are all human beings. Have you ever made the wrong judgement about someone? Or acted stupidly or unfairly? Would you want to be forgiven? Thinking of times when other people forgave you and how positive it felt to be forgiven is a good first step to becoming more empathetic towards others.

Although being empathetic can be very hard when another person has done something very unacceptable, you are doing this to understand their motivation so that you can move on.

must know

Not resolving forgiveness
Deep and on-going distress can be caused when you do not resolve forgiveness issues. Weigh up the long-term benefits of hanging on to your present perceptions and feelings about the situation against the long-term costs.
• Remember that any sympathy you are getting may not continue for ever.
• Remember, too, that when you forgive, your relationships with others get better.
• Understand that forgiveness breeds self-forgiveness which leads to self-acceptance.

7 Anger

Forgiveness ABC model

A – Activating Situation	B - Beliefs	New B - Beliefs required to change the consequences for me	New C- Consequences
What happened? Think about a situation where you feel another person did you a wrong.	What are your automatic thoughts about this situation?	What are the new beliefs you could hold that would change your feelings about the situation and your behaviour?	What will be the emotional, physiological and behavioural consequences for you of adopting these beliefs?
My girlfriend cheated on me.	• It was a terrible thing to do. She is a horrible, nasty person. It wasn't fair. I always treated her well. • I loved her. I will never meet anyone like her again. My life is over.	• Life is sometimes unfair and I can't change that fact. • We are all fallible human beings • I am not happy about the way she behaved towards me but I can survive this. I have survived other things in my life. I was often busy and she was bored and we had stopped communicating so our relationship already had problems. She has said sorry for what happened. She didn't want to hurt me. She can't make my life be over. Only I can choose to do that, or I can choose to let go of the past and move on with my life. Everyone is different and I can learn lessons from what happened and communicate with my new girlfriend better so that we can have a good relationship.	I let go of the anger.

Understanding other people's motivation

Think about what the situation was that hurt you. Can you think of a reason why they acted in the way that they did? Did they intend to harm you? What excuses would they give for their behaviour? Is there even a grain of truth in these excuses?

Each time you put yourself in the mind of another person you are taking a step towards forgiving them so that you can release your pain and anger and have self-acceptance.

Changing your thoughts and feelings

Next go back to your ABC model. Think about how you feel presently and what beliefs are required to hold these unpleasant feelings in place.

Think about how you would like to feel. What thoughts, beliefs, assumptions and evaluations of the situation would you need to have to support new pleasant or neutral feelings about the situation?

Remember that the opposite of a negative feeling is not necessarily an extreme positive reaction, it can simply be calmness or the absence of a strong feeling.

want to know more?
• *Overcoming Anger and irritability*, William Davies, Constable and Robinson, 2000.
• Re-read Chapter 2 on faulty thinking.
• Chapter 11 has advice on self-esteem and self-acceptance.

8 Anxiety

Anxiety affects many of us and an anxiety disorder is a persistent problem for some people. If you have experienced panic attacks or other forms of anxiety this chapter will show you some of the ways in which you can overcome these using CBT.

Anxiety

Everyone gets worried and anxious from time to time. The feeling of worry is similar to one of excitement but accompanied by a sense of unease, apprehension, fear or self-doubt and the anticipation of a threat of some kind. An anxiety disorder, however, is different from an ordinary, occasional feeling of worry because it is both persistent and habitual.

must know

Effects of excessive anxiety
If you suffer from over-worrying or unrealistic anxiety about aspects of your life you may experience some of the following symptoms:
• Feeling unable to cope
• Fear and nervousness
• Feeling of unreality about surroundings
• Performance anxiety
• Expecting others to perceive you or react to you negatively
• Difficulty concentrating
• Racing, obsessive or scary thoughts
• Flashbacks
• Irritability
(continued opposite)

Understanding anxiety

Anxiety comes in several forms. The main first type of anxiety disorder is recurring panic attacks which come out of the blue. In between attacks, you may either feel perfectly OK or you may feel anxious, particularly if you are anticipating when the next panic attack might occur.

The second type of anxiety disorder is worrying excessively and unrealistically about what might be or what is happening to you in your life. This type of anxiety does not include panic attacks.

If you either get anxious about what is happening to you currently or anxious about what could happen to you in the future, the first thing to understand is that it is not the *events* that are triggering your anxiety, it is your *interpretation and anticipation* of them.

If you are anxious, you probably spend a lot of time thinking about all the terrible results and conse-quences to you and those you love of all these things. The more you think about them, the more you gather false evidence for your irrational beliefs and feed the negative anxiety cycle of automatic thoughts and bad feelings.

With depression, these feelings tend to be feelings of loss and sadness or the feeling that you can't do something. If you are anxious, you may feel that bad things will happen to you, and these things are in some way dangerous to you (or the people you love). This might be worry about a perceived physical danger or an emotional threat. The worry appears to be uncontrollable and may interfere with your daily life and your ability to concentrate on day-to-day tasks or just to get on with a normal routine.

Excessive anxiety can affect anyone. However, women statistically experience anxiety-related disorders more than men. Anxiety often co-exists with other negative feelings such as depression. It may also become part of a negative personal cycle of abuse of alcohol, food or drugs.

Overestimating danger

If you get anxious a lot, you will tend to overestimate the threat in a particular situation. Counteracting this perception of a threat means getting a more balanced and realistic view about the likelihood of the danger really happening. If you overestimate danger in your environment it triggers an automatic anxiety programme of responses in your mind and body, as if you have installed a 'start anxiety programme' into a computer.

The automatic anxiety programme

The physical response to danger is for your body to produce adrenalin and prepare for 'fight or flight'. If you were a primitive man on the lookout for an attack by a predator, it would be useful to be automatically on high alert, prepared either to fight

Physical symptoms of anxiety
• Muscle tension, especially in the neck and shoulders
• Twitching
• Nausea
• Frequent urination
• Restlessness
• Chills
• Diarrhoea
• Insomnia, difficulty sleeping, disturbed dreams
• Flushes
• Shaking or trembling hands and legs
• Fatigue
• Breathlessness
• Heart palpitations, pounding and racing
• Dry mouth
• Hot or cold sweats
• Feeling shaky or unsteady
• Lightheadedness

watch out

Up to 6 per cent of people experience an anxiety disorder in one year. Up to 3 per cent of people experience panic attacks in a year.

or run. Even now, it is important at times for the body to go into a state of automatic arousal, where you have an extra energy boost so that you can react quickly. For example, imagine you saw a car about to hit a pram – your adrenalin boost would let you react swiftly to push the pram out of the way. However, if there is no real danger, your physical symptoms will just fuel anxiety. You might feel your heart beating faster as adrenalin is pumped into your system, fuelling a worry that you are having a heart attack.

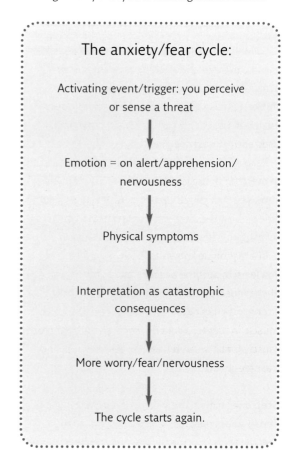

The anxiety/fear cycle:

Activating event/trigger: you perceive or sense a threat

↓

Emotion = on alert/apprehension/ nervousness

↓

Physical symptoms

↓

Interpretation as catastrophic consequences

↓

More worry/fear/nervousness

↓

The cycle starts again.

When the anxiety cycle starts it tends to spiral. An anxiety-prone person interprets physical symptoms and feelings of unease as having the worst possible consequences. By recognizing the symptoms of anxiety and fear as just symptoms, you will stop fuelling your anxiety programme.

Overcoming anxiety

Anxiety disorders can be treated with medication and therapy either separately or in combination. Small lifestyle changes can also have an effect on anxiety levels (see box, right).

CBT is particularly effective. It can be used to help to reduce anxiety by teaching you how to identify, evaluate, control and modify your automatic thinking in response to situations that have set off anxiety in the past. A variety of techniques can be used and are described below.

Relaxation is an effective way to support yourself in overcoming anxiety. It is a way of beginning to show you that you have control over your symptoms. One of the easiest ways to start relaxation is to plan relaxing activities into your daily routines.

In a technique known as Progressive Relaxation, you learn to become aware of and to tense and relax all the muscle groups of your body. This is best done sitting in a chair rather than lying down. Tense each muscle in turn for about five seconds and relax each muscle for between ten and fifteen seconds. This is the order to follow.

Step one: tense and relax technique

Tense your muscles in turn
Feel the tension in the muscle and then let go.

Clench one of your fists so you feel the tension. Bend your arm so you feel the tension all the way up your arm. Clench the other fist and arm. Screw up your face, and your eye muscles. Clench your jaw together. Notice the tension in your throat. Push your chin onto your chest. Hunch your shoulders. Now relax by breathing calmly and deeply from the stomach. Take a big, deep breath, fill up your lungs and exhale.

The rest of the body

As you exhale, pull in your stomach muscles, tensing up the stomach area, tense your buttocks, press your heels into the floor to tense you calves, press your feet and toes down into the floor, pull your toes up to tighten the calves. Now relax and take big, deep breaths through your stomach.

Now rate the level of relaxation you achieved and how long it took you to achieve that level.

With daily practice you will find that it becomes easier to release more tension from your body. Try to do the technique slowly for a total of up to 15 minutes each day.

As soon as you notice progress in your ability to relax quickly, you can move on to a second technique. This time you will just relax each muscle without the need to tense it first as your body will have become used to relaxing.

Step two: release and relax technique

Relax each muscle in your body. Start by relaxing the top of your head and move down through the rest of your head and shoulders, your torso, arms and hands, down through the lower half of your body, and through your legs down to your feet and all the way down to your toes. Let the relaxation spread right down your body with every deep breath you take. Breathe calmly and slowly and as you breathe out, notice any tiny, remaining bits of tension leaving your body. Practise this regularly over a couple of weeks for between five and ten minutes at a time.

Step three: relaxed movement technique

So far you have learned to relax while sitting comfortably in a chair. It is useful after practising this for a few weeks to bring the same levels of relaxation into other environments.

First sit and relax as normal. Notice how quickly you can now get to a deep level of relaxation. Now you can practise adding movement. As you do these movements, scan the body to make sure that you remain relaxed.

• After relaxing, open your eyes, and without moving your head, look at the room you are in. Notice that you can stay relaxed even with your eyes open. Move your head and look around, remaining relaxed.

• Lift one arm or leg, keeping the rest of your body relaxed.

• Practise achieving the same levels of relaxation while walking.

• Practise achieving the same levels of relaxation while standing.

• Practise a different relaxation each day over one to two weeks.

Step four: rapid relaxation

The final stage of relaxation is to be able to relax in just a few seconds. This will enable you to interrupt any anxiety patterns very rapidly. To practise, make sure that you are in a neutral environment.

• First, give yourself a trigger word such as 'relax'. This acts as a reminder to go into relaxation.

• Take three deep breaths. Breathe in slowly.

• Think 'relax' the second before you exhale slowly.

• Check your levels of relaxation. If there are any muscles that you could relax further, just think 'relax' and let the tension out.

To become really proficient at relaxation in any – even a past – anxiety-provoking situation, practise relaxation every day. This could be in the form of meditation, or a simple self-scan of your body so that you notice any tense muscles and deliberately relax them.

Changing your faulty self-talk

Just trying to stop the anxiety cycle without addressing the underlying faulty thinking won't work. An anxious person may say to himself:

- *I must stop this.*
- *It's wrong to feel like this.*
- *I must know if it is serious.*
- *I must not panic or feel anxious.*

This 'must', 'should' and 'ought to' thinking makes him focus on the anxiety and its symptoms. Paying attention to the symptoms makes them go on for longer and appear greater than they may be.

Over time, a person who is particularly anxious may avoid situations that he thinks will trigger discomfort and at the same time may magnify his symptoms in his mind to create other uncomfortable sensations such as fear, hysteria or depression.

The first step to change is to recognize your faulty thinking patterns using your ABC sheets, and challenge them consistently, persuasively and rigorously with new beliefs. By persistently disputing your faulty thinking you will defeat it.

It may take a while to identify your anxiety-related automatic thoughts so keep digging away to uncover the assumptions you are making that set up your personal anxiety cycles.

Anxiety-related pictures

An anxious person may trigger the anxiety through visual mental images. However, these may be so brief he may not even realize at first that they have triggered the negative feeling. Or they may seem

must know

Relaxation reminders
To remind yourself to relax, why not place a colour or symbol on an item at home or at work that you will see regularly – for example, your telephone or fridge door? When you see your trigger, it can act as a reminder to you to scan your body for any tension so that you can rapidly let go of it and relax.

very rational and so it is not obvious that they need to be challenged and disputed. For example, you might see yourself sitting alone at a party you are going to, or being shouted at by the neighbour whom you want to ask to turn their music down. Sometimes the images are very strange but plausible to you – for example, you might see yourself being shouted at by a stranger in the street for going out of your home.

On occasions your automatic thoughts are so ingrained that you may not notice they are there at all, or if a thought enters your mind you quickly try to squash it by escaping from the trigger situation as quickly as possible.

It is important to capture these habitual thoughts so that you can work through the ABC sheets and overcome this way of thinking for once and for all, rather than simply avoiding certain situations.

By practising new ways of thinking and by persuading yourself to take new actions and confront what you are afraid of head on, you turn your personal dragons into mice – diminishing or extinguishing your worries and fears.

Habituation – overcoming avoidance

If you are worried about something, you may well try to avoid the situation which you think will trigger the anxiety. Unfortunately, by avoiding the situation you are anxious about, you will only reinforce your negative thoughts about it. It is important to expose yourself very gradually to the situation you are afraid of and stay in it until your anxiety starts to decrease. This process is known as habituation. Each time you face a fear, it gets weaker.

must know

Useful thinking
Although it would be nice never to be upset or have things go wrong, you are a human being. Things will happen to you. Worrying about them won't ever cure them or make them go away.

must know

Challenging automatic anxiety-provoking thoughts

Ask yourself:
• What evidence do I have for this thought?
• Is there an alternative way of looking at this situation?
• How would someone else look at this situation?
• Am I being over-perfectionist and setting myself standards that are too high and too difficult to reach?
• Am I being black and white/all-or-nothing in my thinking?
• Am I over-focusing on some facts and ignoring others?
• Am I over-personalizing – taking too much responsibility for this situation?
• Am I overestimating how much I can control this situation?
• Am I underestimating how many resources I have to deal with the situation?
• Am I overestimating how likely the outcome that I am worried about is?
• What will I feel in a year or so when it is all over?

Anxiety rating record

Keep a record of how successful your experiments are:
• Write down *before* you put yourself in the situation your current predictions about it: what you fear may happen including any catastrophic consequences – your worst fears.
• Now rate on a scale of 0–10 how anxious or uncomfortable you think the situation will be for you when you are in it.
• Next, see what actually does happen. *After* the event, rate on a scale of 0–10 your actual levels of anxiety and discomfort. Also, note down for how long you exposed yourself to the trigger situation.

What anxious people generally discover is that they can accurately estimate how anxious they will be in certain circumstances but they overestimate the negative consequences. The catastrophes they were afraid of rarely happen.

It is important that you expose yourself to trigger situations only in a very managed, graded way, so it may require the support of a therapist. If you expose yourself too quickly, you will simply be overwhelmed and may just want to get out of the situation as quickly as possible. On the other hand, too little exposure will simply be ineffective as you will not see enough progress to overcome your old negative beliefs and replace them with new ones.

Anxiety disorders

This section focuses on some of the other common anxiety disorders you may come across. These are many and varied and it is important that you do get in touch with a therapist and your doctor if you are suffering from phobias or obsessional disorders.

Panic attacks

Recurrent panic attacks are a sign of an anxiety state. Some are preceded by a build-up of anxiety. Others appear to come out of the blue.

A panic attack may take the form of a feeling of apprehension about impending danger followed by physical symptoms including chest pains or palpitations, choking, dizziness, weakness in the legs, ringing in the ears, tingling or sweating, chills and breathlessness.

Some people who have panic attacks may think they are about to have a heart attack or just have a feeling of unreality and a feeling that they are losing control or even that they are going mad.

The danger with panic attacks is that the person who has one misinterprets it as being genuinely dangerous and then sets up a spiral of further anxiety triggering more physical symptoms.

Do you need to remain a victim of panic attacks? Definitely not – use your ABC sheets to challenge your thinking and use gradual exposure to anxiety situations to modify and change your reactions. Creating your own behavioural experiments will allow you to realize that the catastrophes you predict are false.

Phobias

A phobia is a fear that builds up around a trigger situation, object, animal or person. The trigger is not really dangerous but even when the person recognizes that their reaction is not rational they still

watch out

Check for avoidance behaviour
• Are you avoiding situations because you are anxious or afraid of what will happen?
• Are there things you don't do any more because you are anxious or afraid or what will happen?
• Are there things you stop doing when you notice anxiety starting?

experience fear and discomfort. The symptoms of a phobia are:
• **Physiological:** fast heart rate, trembling, fast, shallow breathing, shaking, sweating, muscle tension, weak legs, feeling sick or nervous in the stomach.
• **Behavioural:** freezing or moving to escape as quickly as possible – jumping out of the way.
• **Subjective:** symptoms that vary from individual to individual, e.g. anger, shame, feelings of failure.

Treatment for phobias is once again based around the idea of gradual desensitization to trigger situations. Whether the phobia is simple or complex, it is assumed that the behaviour can be unlearned because it was learned to begin with. By 'facing down the fear' of what triggers the fear, the phobic learns that the fear is groundless.

Agoraphobia
Agoraphobics' anxiety is triggered by a fear of being outside or specifically being away from a place of safety, generally the home. Fear may be triggered by the distance from safety or by being in an unfamiliar place such as public transport. Some agoraphobics have a fear of confined spaces as well. They may be afraid of generally panicking, fainting or not being able to escape in a hurry.

To overcome agoraphobia, it is important to overcome your safety and avoidance behaviours with measured and gradual exposure to trigger situations. Keep a practice record of your progress.

Social phobia
Social phobics are worried about what other people will think of them. They are concerned that they will be negatively evaluated, criticized and rejected. As a result they avoid social situations because they assume that they will be met with at

the least an unfriendly reaction and at worst other catastrophic consequences including loss of control. The best way to deal with this phobia is once again to carry out behavioural

Practice record

Example goal: to go to the post office or shop once a day			
Day/what I did	Anticipated anxiety (0-10)	Actual anxiety level (0-10)	Symptoms
Wed/Walked to a shop 100 yards away to buy a newspaper.	7	5	Shaking hands; felt weak in the legs.

experiments – test out your worst predictions to disprove them and to challenge your negative thoughts, particularly catastrophizing. It is also useful to learn to direct your attention outwards to the other people you encounter rather than to keep your attention focused inwards, since that will keep you highlighting and fuelling your own fears.

Obessive-compulsive disorder (OCD)

Obsessions are unwanted and upsetting thoughts and urges triggered by different events and stimuli. Everybody experiences some degree of obsession – for example, the need to go back and double check. However an obsession is a problem when it starts to interfere with your daily life. CBT is recognized as a very effective intervention for OCDs.

Obsessives experience:

• **Feelings of anxiety and discomfort**, sometimes including a feeling that they should be resisting the compulsion to carry out a certain behaviour.

• **Compulsive or *neutralizing* behaviour,** where they do perform an action according to set rules they have given yourselves – a ritual – to relieve their anxiety levels.

• **Avoidance behaviours,** where they avoid certain situations

Common obsessions
• Fear of harming self or others accidentally or on purpose.
• Preoccupation with death.
• Fear of sex or committing unacceptable sexual acts, e.g. rape.
• Fear of contamination, e.g. being harmed by contact with dirt, urine, germs, blood, etc.
• Need to check orderliness; things need to be done in the right order, a certain way, or arranged in the right order.
• Religious obsession, e.g fear of committing blasphemy.
• Fear of committing socially unacceptable behaviour, e.g. losing control, swearing.

and stimuli so that they don't set off obsessional thoughts.

A therapist dealing with a patient with OCD will take a detailed history about the nature and duration of the problem as well as a full description of the thoughts that accompany it, the emotional content and behavioural triggers and avoidance/ safety behaviours. The main treatments for OCD are to expose the patient to situations they have previously avoided and stimuli they are afraid of, and to prevent them from using their compulsive rituals and neutralizing behaviours. Generally, a therapist will set short-, medium- and long-term targets for the treatment.

Monitoring your progress

It is always important to keep a check on your progress to see how effectively you are changing your thinking and feeling patterns.

Diaries

You can use a daily diary or record sheet to keep a check on your symptoms. An example is given on page 147 for panic attacks. Write down the situation and when it occurred on one side of the page. Assess the severity of your reaction to the situation and your immediate thoughts about it.

On your record sheet, keep a check on how your belief in your thoughts is changing as well. To do this, it is useful to rate how strongly you believe in a particular thought with 0 equalling 'no belief' and 10 equalling 'I totally believe this thought'.

Rate both your belief in the first irrational thoughts that accompanied the anxiety and then after you have come up with a more rational response, look back at the original thoughts and re-rate your response to them. Finally rate your level of belief in the new rational thoughts.

Acquiring new skills

On occasion, a lack of skills may be at the heart of why a person gets anxious about a future situation. For example, you may not have the communication skills for a party or a work situation and so you become anxious when facing these types of situations. If this is the case, you may be able to learn new skills through role play with a therapist or through skills courses.

want to know more?
• *Overcoming Anxiety*, Helen Kennerley, Constable and Robinson, 1997
• **For online materials on anxiety and related disorders Anxiety Network International www.anxietynetwork. com/index.html**
• **The Obsessive Compulsive Foundation www.ocfoundation.org**
• **The National Centre for PTSD (post-traumatic stress disorder) www.ncptsd. org/index. html**

Practice record

Trigger situation: *When? Where?*	Wednesday. 10am
Physical symptoms	Palpitations. Tightness in the chest. Slight sweating. Breathing fast and shallow...
How severe were symptoms 1-10	8/10
Automatic thoughts *Immediate interpretation of the incident – negative response*	I can't go on. I am going to faint.
Rate belief in these thoughts 1-10	9/10
Rational response *Re-evaluated positive response – resetting your beliefs*	It's just overload and anxiety because I am dealing with too many things in one go. If I say 'stop' to myself and count to ten my breathing will slow.
Re-rate belief in negative automatic thoughts. 1-10	3/10
Finally, rate belief in rational response. 1-10	9/10

9 Depression

Cognitive Behavioural Therapy for depression is one of the most widely evaluated and adopted treatments for this disorder. This chapter looks at specific ways you can overcome depression using CBT.

Depression

A person who is depressed feels extreme mental anguish. Clinical depression has been diagnosed so widely that it is sometimes referred to as the common cold of psychiatry.

must know

Efficacy
The Royal College of Psychiatrists says that CBT is 'the most effective psychological treatment for moderate and severe depression; as effective as antidepressants for many types of depression'.

Feeling depressed

About 20 per cent of us are estimated to experience some symptoms of depression at any one time. Among women in Western societies the rate is double that of men, according to research in the 1970s.

As the English poet John Milton (1608–74) put it,

The mind is its own place, and in itself can make a Heav'n of Hell, a Hell of Heav'n.

The symptoms of depression

In this chapter, depression will be used to refer to non-bipolar and non-psychotic depressive disorders.

Depression can range in strength from mild to severe. However, a clinically depressed person will experience identifiable symptoms over a period of two weeks or more. This is different from the short-term, transient mood swings that many people suffer because of loss or a bad event.

Depressed people may become tearful, feel sad, may experience guilt and be irritable. Some may find it difficult to get out of bed, have very low energy or have numbed emotions. Some may find that they can't even watch TV or read because they are unable to focus. In general, depression limits the ability of the person to enjoy day-to-day life.

At its worth, the depressed person may have a preoccupation with suicide. Sufferers of severe depression over many years say that they would do anything to escape the severity of the mental anguish they experience.

Antidepressant medication will help some depressed people. Others will benefit from a course of CBT alone or a mixture of medication and CBT. If you find that your normal life is being disrupted by symptoms of depression then it is recommended that you ask your doctor for advice.

How depression develops

Depression is triggered in line with the same ABC model as other emotions, according to CBT research. In other words, people's experiences lead them to make assumptions about themselves and the world.

This then determines how they behave and how they evaluate events and their own behaviour. Some of the assumptions they make are rigid or irrational and become counterproductive, fuelling negative emotions.

Each time an irrational assumption is triggered it will unleash automatic negative thoughts about what is happening currently and what will happen in the future as well as what has happened in the past.

This then leads to symptoms of depression:
• Emotional, e.g. anxiety
• Motivational, e.g. inertia
• Physical, e.g. loss of sleep
• Cognitive, e.g. poor memory
• Behavioural, e.g. withdrawal

Example of a depression vicious circle

Early experience sets up irrational assumptions

(A parent leaves home when you are a child – there is a lack of support and love in the house and lack of acknowledgement of your worth as a person. Assumptions are set up: I am worth little; people will reject or leave me unless I am nice to them and do what they want.)

↓

Critical incident

(Major relationship breaks down. At the same time you are made redundant.)

↓

Assumptions triggered

↓

Negative automatic thoughts

(I am a failure. I made this happen. My life is worthless. I will be alone my whole life. People always reject me. My life is a disaster.)

↓

Symptoms of depression

- Emotional: guilt, shame, sadness
- Motivational: loss of interest in previously pleasurable activities, inability to do day-to-day tasks
- Physical: difficulty getting to sleep, loss of appetite, self-neglect
- Cognitive: self-criticism, rumination, inability to make decisions
- Behavioural: withdrawal from friends and family, little activity

Researchers recognize that depression may have a number of causes including biological, social and psychological factors. However, changing your unconscious thinking patterns will still act as an effective intervention whatever the cause.

The vicious cycle of depression

• If you are depressed, you think more negative automatic thoughts, more frequently and more intensely, crowding out other more rational thoughts as the depression grows.

• At the same time, the more depressed thoughts you think, the more you believe them and the more depressed you become.

Rumination

Rumination is when you worry and go over problems again and again in your head. These thoughts are intrusive and involuntary but do not solve the problem in question.

Rumination is a key part of sustaining depression. The person focuses on how bad the situation is and how bad they feel about it. They may ask questions such as, 'Why has this happened to me?' Or make statements such as, 'I should have done XYZ'. Or, 'if only XYZ had happened it would all have been OK.'

What doesn't work

These types of question don't solve the automatic thinking pattern. The person may also 'try' not to have bad thoughts through avoidance. This does not work as the thinking errors have not been effectively challenged. What won't work either is for the depressed person to focus on happy topics. Why?

Symptoms of clinical depression

If you have three or more of these symptoms for over two weeks, you should consult your doctor.

• Numb emotions – inability to feel strongly
• Indecisiveness
• Anxiety
• Irritability
• Rumination – going over and over past problems or questions without answer
• Lack of concentration
• Loss of libido/sexual desire
• Negative thoughts about self – beliefs about own worthlessness
• Negative thoughts about the world as an unsafe or unpleasant place
• Insomnia/disturbed sleep – finding it difficult to get to sleep, waking up too soon, or oversleeping
• Comfort eating/overeating or loss of appetite
• Poor memory
• Loss of enjoyment of day-to-day activities, feeling you can't face the day ahead
• Social withdrawal - avoiding interactions and seeing other people
• Neglecting appearance
• Neglecting to take care of home environment
• Fearing the future, feelings of hopelessness - that there is no end to this state
• Reduced activity levels
• Feelings of guilt
• Suicidal thoughts, longing for death or thinking 'it doesn't matter whether I live or die'

Because the beliefs and assumptions the person is making about himself that are feeding the negative thought and emotion cycle still exist. If he believes he is a failure, worthless and stupid he won't eradicate that basic belief by thinking about happy things. Only once the belief is eliminated can the depressive symptoms be got rid of.

Interrupting your ruminations

You can interrupt your rumination patterns by:
• using your ABC sheets (to challenge the false, irrational beliefs and to replace them with more rational beliefs)
• distraction techniques (finding an alternative to focus on reduces the amount of negative thoughts)
• scheduling activity (doing something to keep yourself busy – in particular exercise – will keep ruminations at bay).

Four distraction techniques

These techniques are effective in stopping the amount of time you spend ruminating. They do not change your thought patterns permanently but they can stop the build-up of a vicious circle of thinking.

1. Sensory awareness: focus on what is happening right now. Look at your environment. Become aware of your sight, hearing, touch, smell and taste. This brings you back from selective negative filtering to a more positive interaction with your environment. Ask yourself:
• What do you notice around you? What else?
• What can you hear?
• What can you see?
• What can you taste?

Negative depressive thought patterns
These tend to revolve around three areas.
1. The self: e.g. *I am a failure*
2. The current situation: e.g. *Whatever I try doesn't work.*
3. The future: e.g. *This is never going to get better.*

Depressive automatic thinking patterns have a number of common characteristics.
• They are automatic and involuntary.
• They are habitual.
• They are plausible.
• They are triggered by an extensive range of stimuli.

• What can you smell?
• What are you touching?
• What does your clothing feel like?

2 Mental distraction: think about an object in your environment. Look at it and focus in on the detail. Describe it to yourself in as much detail as possible.
• What shape is it?
• What colour is it?
• What is it made of?
• What other details do you notice about it?

3 Counting sheep: count backwards from 300 to 1, recite the letters of the alphabet, count the number of animals you can think of beginning with 's' – any mental task that keeps your focus on facts is helpful.

4 Endorphin raising: thinking about something pleasurable you have done in the past immediately raises the endorphin level in your body. Have ready to bring to mind a picture or image that always makes you smile, a memory of a past holiday you loved or a favourite place. It is a good idea to make a list of ten or so happy images so that you can bring them to mind at any moment to disrupt negative thought patterns. It is helpful too to relive pleasant experiences in detail. Remember where you were, what you were doing – as if you are running a film through your mind.

Activity works
Activity acts as a mood elevator. Withdrawing, staying in bed and staying away from normal social activities act as mood depressants. Scheduling and monitoring activity levels to make sure that they are sustained is a useful step towards breaking the vicious cycle of depression.

To break your inactivity cycle, it is useful to keep a record sheet so that you can plan every day and at the same time build up gradually from inactivity to activity.

Start by recording what you are doing now on an hour-by-hour basis. Write in every activity you do – from getting up and making breakfast to washing up, shopping, watching TV, talking to a friend on the telephone or going to the cinema.

Next, start to plan in some activities. Remember to build up your activity level gradually.

It is useful to rate each activity out of ten in terms of the pleasure it gave you (P) and also (M) mastery – the sense of achievement you felt in doing it. There's an example plan below and overleaf you will find a blank plan that you can photocopy and use to record your own activities.

must know

Keeping a diary
Some people like to keep a diary as part of their goal-setting process. It allows you to get your thoughts and feelings on to paper and is a useful stress release as well as a measurement system for looking at your progress against your goals. Be careful to give credit to your achievements and the real progress you make.

Example of activity record sheet

	Monday	Tuesday	Wednesday	Thursday	Friday
8-10 a.m.	Got up, had breakfast (P0, M2)	Got up, had breakfast (P1, M2)	Washed up (P1, M3)	Got up and listened to radio (P4, M4)	Got up and listened to radio (P4, M4)
10-12 a.m.	Fed cat (P0, M2)	Rang my mother (P2, M5)	Drove to work (P4, M5)	Drove to work and gave friend a lift (P4, M5)	Went for a walk (P5, M6)

Activity plan

	Monday	Tuesday	Wednesday
6-8 a.m.			
8-10			
10-12			
12-2			
2-4			
4-6			
6-8			
8-10			
10-12 p.m			

Thursday	Friday	Saturday	Sunday

Mood-rating diary

To check your progress generally, it can be useful to keep a daily mood-rating diary (see also previous mood diary example on page 101).

Each day, estimate how depressed you have been on a scale of 0 to 100 per cent. Over several weeks, as you use the CBT methods you may find your diary will end up looking something like this:

	Week 1	Week 2	Week 3	Week 4	Week 5
Monday	50%	50%	40%	30%	0%
Tuesday	70%	50%	40%	20%	10%
Wednesday	70%	50%	30%	0%	0%
Thursday	60%	60%	30%	10%	0%
Friday	50%	40%	50%	0%	20%
Saturday	80%	60%	30%	10%	0%
Sunday	80%	60%	40%	30%	10%

Common thinking errors

Common thinking errors that trigger negative automatic thoughts in depression (see Chapter 2).

• Personalization: my friend hasn't rung me. It must be because I am negative.

• Overgeneralization: for example, making one mistake and assuming that it means that everything will now fail.

• Mental filtering: only noticing the negative in the situation. 'The whole day was depressing' – failing to notice the activities during the day which were pleasurable.

• Black and white, all-or-nothing thinking: 'I can't get everything right today so I might as well give up.'

• Irrational inference: drawing a conclusion based on one instance: 'I didn't manage to fill in the activity

schedule so the therapy will be a failure.'
• 'Must' thinking. 'I must have a relationship. I don't so I am a failure.'
• Expectations of negative outcomes: 'I can't do it now, I haven't been able to do it in the past, I won't be able to do it in the future.'
• Expectations and feelings of loss and sadness: 'I have lost everything in my life.'
• Feelings of being out of control: 'My memory is going. I can't focus on anything.'

Challenging negative thought patterns

As with any disorder, you can use the ABC sheets in Chapter 5 to challenge your negative automatic thoughts and their underlying assumptions.

If you are depressed, it may not be easy either to distance yourself enough from your feelings to be rational about them or to get the energy to fill in the sheets. If you experience this, it is probably helpful to work on them with a therapist first of all rather than on your own and also to limit the time you spend on thought-challenging activities.

Here are some steps you can take to help you fill in your sheets:

• **Identify the emotions you are experiencing.** As soon as you start feeling your mood drop and become more negative it is a signal that there are automatic thoughts there. If you catch them at this point you can stop these thoughts becoming ruminations. Write down the emotions in section C of an ABC sheet. Rate your emotions for intensity on a scale of 0–100. This will allow you to measure any changes you make through challenging your thoughts.

must know

Identifying negative thoughts
If you can't identify these thoughts easily, ask yourself: 'What did this situation mean to me? What did it tell me about myself, now and in the future?'

• **Identify the situation that started the thoughts.** Write down a description of it in the A section of your ABC sheet. Describe what you were doing, e.g. I was talking to my wife.

• **Identify the automatic thoughts.** Write down in the B section of your ABC sheet what went through your head as you began to feel low. Now rate how much you believe each thought on a 0-100 rating. Make sure when you write down what you thought you record in as much detail as possible not only the thoughts but also any images that came into your head. Make sure you have got the underlying thoughts as well as the initial ones. For example, if you leave your keys in the car and find yourself getting very depressed, what is really setting off the feeling? The initial thought – I made a mistake? Or an underlying assumption, I am a failure – I never get anything right? Make sure you match the intensity of the emotion to the thought. Check: 'if I thought this, would I feel this bad?' If the answer is no, then you need to check your underlying assumptions.

Dispute and challenge your thoughts and assumptions until you win! To fill in the rest of the ABC forms, ask yourself for a rational response to your irrational thinking. Your goal is to debate with yourself until you end up winning!

• What is the evidence for this?

• What thinking errors am I making? (See Chapter 2.)

• What are the advantages and disadvantages of this way of thinking?

• In what way is the assumption I am making unreasonable/ irrational?

• In what way is the assumption I am making unhelpful?

• Where does this assumption come from (e.g. could it really belong to the thinking of my parents, not me)?

• Is there an alternative way of looking at/thinking about this that would give me the advantages of the old way of thinking without the disadvantages?

Example thought record

A. I'm feeling depressed and sad again about my relationship and everything. It started when I went out for the evening and she paid attention to someone else.

B. Automatic thoughts: we are not going to survive as a couple because I am too negative. I *should* have had a committed, successful relationship by now, and I am too old. I *must* know why I am so bad at relationships, or else I'll never have a successful relationship. I *shouldn't* have made mistakes in relationships in the past but I did, so I will always fail in relationships.

   Assumption: no one wants me. I am incapable of forming an ongoing relationship because I am a failure and unlovable. (Rating of strength of belief in thoughts: 80–90 per cent)

C. I am sleeping badly. I feel empty and alone (rating of emotions: 90 per cent severity).

D. Dispute your thoughts. The challenge to the thoughts will need to be rigorous to destroy the existing beliefs and supposed evidence for them. When we have deeply held beliefs they tend to be supported by a cluster of other beliefs and so can be resistant to change or challenge initially. The only way is to keep challenging until you win the argument with yourself.

Response

E. Effective new thinking. How much you believe in each statement (? per cent).

• I can't change what has happened in the past (100 per cent).

• I am a human being and therefore fallible (50 per cent).

• I still have time to experiment with new ways of doing things (40 per cent).

• People often fail and then succeed at something after years of failing (50 per cent).
• There's no point constantly thinking about mistakes in the past (80 per cent).
• Things can change in the future (40 per cent).
• There is no proof that because I have failed in the past I will fail in the future (90 per cent).
• There is no 'must' as to how or when I have a relationship (50 per cent). Maybe in the past, I have not ended relationships I knew were wrong early enough because I wanted a relationship too much (60 per cent) and because I didn't like conflict (70 per cent). A good relationship doesn't have to be perfect (60 per cent).
• If I go out to new places and meet different types of people maybe I will have different types of relationships (70 per cent).
Now check: how much do you believe the thoughts (50 per cent) and how do you rate your feelings now (40 per cent)? What can you do now?

Conducting new belief experiments

Once you have challenged your old ways of thinking with new possible beliefs, it is time to put them to the test. Never assume how people will react to you, find out through experimentation. The key is to write everything down!

Step 1 Predict what you think will happen: e.g. if I tell my boss what I feel about doing that work he won't be happy with me.

Step 2 Look at evidence for existing predictions. Look at contradictory evidence.

Step 3 Experiment to test your predictions in a way to maximize the likelihood of a positive outcome. Note down the results.

Step 4 Learn from the results. Do another experiment.

A final word

Setting clear goals for yourself to overcome depression will give you the motivation to overcome it. Some people who are depressed find the idea of goals overpowering at first. If this is the case, your first action should be to go to your doctor for an accurate diagnosis of clinical depression and recommended treatment. That will be a major achievement for your first goal.

Others go to the opposite extreme, thinking that overcoming depressive thoughts will take no time at all. False hope of instant success will just send you down the depression spiral again, so give yourself time to change and set yourself goals.

To beat depression, break your goals down into reasonable targets in three areas:

• Physical
• Emotional
• Mental

View each activity you do as a manageable step towards change, helping you to build a more positive mindset and allowing you to make real progress.

Support

If you are not sure how to do this by yourself, ask for input from a therapist or from your family or friends. Let yourself off the hook if you do not reach all your goals. Always keep in mind that you are a fallible human being. Slow down if necessary. It is better to make slow progress than no progress.

When you reach a goal, remember to reward yourself. Give yourself a treat. Acknowledge and appreciate the progress you have made.

want to know more?
• For more information on depression this is an excellent online resource –
Beyond Blue: The National Depression Initiative
www.beyondblue.org.au
• The Mood Gym –
moodgym.anu.edu.au is an Australian-based CBT website for use with depression.
• Chapter 2 has advice on faulty thinking.
• Read Chapter 7 for more about anger.

10 Stress and tension

Stress is a very individual reaction to a trigger event and comes out of how we perceive events. Most stress is caused from what goes on inside – not outside – us. In this chapter we look at common triggers to stress and how to challenge the faulty thinking patterns which lead to feelings of stress.

Stress and tension

Stress is natural. Ever since primitive man walked the earth there have been challenges to face and stresses to stretch us and compel us to grow. Stress can be welcome and helpful or unwelcome and unhelpful.

Modern life and stress

Positive stress is when you experience a pressure to take an action that you find stimulating and challenging. However, not all stress is good for you. Negative stress is debilitating. It happens when the pressure is too great and you feel there are too many demands on you at any one time.

Is stress increasing? The common view is that modern life is full of more stresses than life in the past, but is that really true?

The modern worker faces stresses from the volume of work produced by our 24/7 culture, commuting on crowded trains and difficult colleagues. A modern parent feels that their life is at a faster pace than in previous decades.

Chronic stress does appear to be increasing in certain professions. More and more people are experiencing anxiety, insomnia and irritability as well as health problems. But there are others in exactly the same situations who retain their sense of humour, keep their high energy levels and are generally happy with their lives, living apparently stress-free.

Stress is defined differently by different professions. A useful way of thinking about stress is to think of it as a demand placed on your mental and physical capacities.

must know

Different views of stress
It is important to realize that correlation is not the same as causation. If you think differently about an event from another person, you will experience a different amount of stress. Through CBT you can learn to address your automatic thoughts triggered by 'stressful situations'.

Stress is always a perception. Some people feel stress when they are in jobs that they are bored by. Other people feel stress around a demanding partner or boss. Some people might get stressed at the idea that they have a party to organize. Each of these situations is stressful only in the eye of the beholder.

If you believe you have the capacity to deal with the demand then you will not feel stressed. If you do not believe that you have the capacity to cope with the demands placed on you, then you will feel stressed.

The stress mismatch

In essence stress is a mismatch between how you view the demands on you and what you believe you have available to you in terms of resources and abilities.

If you change your view about the situation you face you will overcome the stress. Alternatively, if you change your view about the resources you have available to you, you will overcome the stress.

If you have made an accurate assessment of the demands and resources on you, you may still find a lack of match between the two sides. However, you can change this situation by asking for help or looking for extra skills training to bridge the gap. The key is that in each situation you have an opportunity for change – you can either change the situation, or if that choice is not available, you can change your response.

Perception

1. How stress is produced

Perceived demand on you/threat

versus

Perceived resources available to cope with demand

=

Imbalance

Stress

(Behavioural, emotional, physiological reactions)

2. Overturning stress

Rational assessment of demand on you/threat

versus

Rational assessment of resources available to cope with demand

=

Balance

Positive stress

(Behavioural, emotional, physiological reactions)

The effects of stress

The perceived threats we are confronted with today are different from those faced by our hunter-gatherer ancestors. They had to deal with danger from wild animals or enemies. Our physiology developed so that we could run away in a hurry from this type of threat by initiating the fight or flight response.

Fight or flight

Your body makes no distinction between a physical or a psychological threat. Biology takes over as soon as a threat is sensed, mobilizing your automatic nervous system. This controls your heartbeat and internal organs and at the same time it also controls your emotions.

When your automatic nervous system goes into alarm mode it is known as fight or flight. Your body's defences are triggered – your breathing gets shallower, your reflexes are sharpened and adrenalin is released into the body. You are ready to run away from your aggressor.

With a more modern threat, this arousal response is still there but when you don't run away, you are just left with the symptoms. The situation is unresolved but the physical changes in your body are still there. Since modern life involves many potential psychological threats much of your stress can be ongoing and continuing stress symptoms can have a debilitating effect on your life and your physical health.

Your stress potential

Each of us has a different 'stress potential' based on how our self-talk causes us to react in different ways to similar situations.

Change

Some situations are very likely to act as activating events, triggering stress in many people. Changes to routines, for example – even happy ones such as marriage – may be stressful.

must know

Recognizing the behavioural signs of stress

• Inability to concentrate
• Avoiding people
• Less interest in sex
• Deterioration of short- and long-term memory
• Slower response speeds
• Inability to plan and organize
• Increase in hypochondria
• Changes in personality
• Increase in physical and psychological tensions
• Increase in mistakes
• Falling self-esteem
• Inability to concentrate
• Shorter attention span
• Procrastination – shifting responsibility onto others
• Loss of passion and enthusiasm for things previously interested in
• Substance and alcohol abuse
• 'Strange' behaviour
• Cynicism about life and other people

The process of change is sometimes shown as a curve. According to the work of Rosabeth Moss Kanter, we go through different stages.

• The first is **denial** – at the early stage of change a typical reaction may be to disbelieve it has happened.

• The next stage is **emotion** – you may experience grief at losing the situation which has just passed. You may feel angry, sad or frustrated.

• Next comes **resistance** – if you are resistant to change, unhelpful behaviours may come out. You may try to fight the change or be blaming of other people involved. You may well feel very stressed if you stick at this stage.

• **Acceptance** follows but there is no set time frame for this. Many people will begin to accept change and realize its inevitability. Optimists will see that change may be very good for them. Perhaps it is not all bad and there may be ways of making the most of it.

• The final stage is **commitment** – at this point you are prepared to go with the change; you start to see its benefits and you are committed to taking steps to make sure it goes ahead.

Stress and illness

The Holmes-Rahe social readjustment scale is the best-known study of the effects of change and the links of stress to illness. Holmes and Rahe based their well-used scale on research they carried out on 5,000 patients who had suffered from recent illness. Their aim was to understand whether or not life events could lead to illness in the body. On questioning patients they found that many had experienced major life events in the period leading to their illness. Holmes and Rahe concluded that the changes associated with life events use up energy and therefore reduce the body's capacity to prevent illness. Other studies since have supported the idea that stress or even focusing on negative emotions or events can have some correlation with illness. The Holmes-Rahe Social Adjustment Scale in reproduced on page 174.

Stress and faulty thinking patterns

A number of research studies have concluded that there is a link between your thoughts and the amount of stress you experience.

As with other unwanted feelings, faulty thinking patterns and negative self-talk can help to create stress. Uncovering these will help you to keep your fears in proportion and to turn difficulties into opportunities.

The most common faulty thinking patterns are given below. However, it is important to realize that other beliefs that are very personal to you may be at the heart of your stress, so spend time identifying your particular patterns.

1. Perfectionism/all-or-nothing thinking

A perfectionist 'has' to get it 100 per cent right. They never feel that they have achieved the success they really want and expect because they have set themselves impossible standards. As a result they neither appreciate their achievements nor can ever relax because they have attained a goal completely. Perfectionism is based on irrational beliefs because it does not accept the fallibility of real people in real situations. If you are perfectionist, there is always

must know

Recognizing the emotional signs of stress
• Feeling irritable
• Depression and helplessness
• Loss of confidence
• Agitation
• Worrying

must know

Recognizing the physiological signs of stress
• Low energy levels
• Disrupted sleep
• Heart racing
• Cold sweats
• Tingling in fingers and toes
• Dry mouth
• Butterflies
• Tight, shallow breathing
• Tiredness
• Muscle tension
• Backache
• Physical sickness
• Headaches

The Holmes-Rahe Social Readjustment Scale

Life Events	Crisis Units	Life Events	Crisis Units
Death of a spouse	100	Foreclosure of mortgage or loan	30
Divorce	73	Change of responsibilities at work	29
Marital separation	65	Trouble with in-laws	29
Jail term or prosecution	63	Outstanding personal achievement	28
Death of a close family member	63	Husband/wife begins or stops work	26
Personal injury or illness	53	Beginning or ending school	26
Marriage	50	Change in living conditions	25
Losing job	47	Revision of personal habits	24
Marital reconciliation	45	Trouble with boss	23
Retirement	45	Change in work hours or conditions	20
Change in health of family member	44	Change in recreation	19
Pregnancy	40	Change in Church activities	19
Sex difficulties	39	Change in social activities	18
Gain of a new family member	39	Change in sleeping habits	16
Business readjustment	39	Change in number of family	
Change of a financial state	38	get-togethers	15
Death of a close friend	37	Change in eating habits	15
Change in different line of work	36	Vacation	13
Change in number of arguments		Christmas	12
with spouse	35	Minor violations of the law	11

Key (Holmes-Rahe interpretation of the scale)

1–150	No significant problems
150–199	Mild life crisis (33 per cent chance of illness)
200–299	Moderate life crisis (50 per cent chance of illness)
300 or over	Major life crisis (80 per cent chance of illness)

Watch Out: This scale is just to give you an indication of the range of stressful factors you may encounter; there may be a number of events not included in the list that you personally find particularly stressful. Use the scale instead to help you to identify stressful trigger situations that you can challenge using CBT.

something else you could have done, you are always an inch away from perfect success, which may mean that you feel you have failed. This belief then triggers stress.

If you have a tendency to think pessimistically, you can increase your optimistic thinking through the gratitude technique (see box, right).

2. Personalization

If you tend to take responsibility for everything that happens in situations be careful – you may be taking on stress unnecessarily.

If you accept too much responsibility, challenge your thinking. Think about the situation that has triggered your stress. Who else is involved? How much are you really responsible for this situation? What responsibility belongs to others? What else could other people do?

3. Pessimism

Pessimistic thinking is a major trigger for stress. Research on optimism and pessimism shows that pessimism has effects on ageing, general health, happiness and even the immune system. Optimistic people have better general health and outlive their pessimistic colleagues.

Allow for fallibility: apply the 80/20 rule. If you achieve 80 per cent of what you set out to do, give yourself a pat on the back.

Reward even small successes. Eliminate all-or-nothing thinking. Remember, one positive action, however small, is a step forwards.

must know

The gratitude technique
Each day just before you go to bed, write down three things you are pleased and grateful for that day. These can be very small things:
• I am grateful that the postman smiled at me today
• I am pleased that I had an enjoyable shopping expedition today
• I am pleased that I got the washing-up done today.
Then write down what you did to make those situations happen. What was your contribution? This is a very effective technique to produce more positive thinking habits.

Beliefs linked to procrastination
• I will have to complete the task in one go.
• I don't like it and so I can't do it.
• I can only do it if I am in a certain mood.
• Tasks should be interesting for one to do them.
• I have lots of time left.
• I will do it better if I leave myself hardly any time to do it. The deadline will help me finish the task.
• I can't do it perfectly yet. I don't have all the information I need so I had better wait.
• I might need to change what I do later so there is no point starting now.

4. Procrastination

The word 'procrastinate' comes from the Latin meaning 'for tomorrow'. When you procrastinate you put off an action until later. Stress levels tend to be raised when you do this. While stress is an emotional problem, procrastination is a behavioural one. Nevertheless, they are both triggered by faulty beliefs. Unreasonable procrastination can also be linked to other uncomfortable emotions such as depression and anxiety.

Although procrastination is not necessarily always a poor or unreasonable choice, if you start to experience discomfort around it, it is worth tackling the underlying thoughts.

Combating procrastination will help you to overcome many sources of future stress. For example, if you finish that work paper now, in two weeks' time you won't panic about the fact that you only have a day left to do it.

Challenge your beliefs to defeat procrastination

• Irrational Belief: *'This isn't enjoyable therefore I can't/shouldn't do it now.'*
Challenge: *'This isn't particularly enjoyable but if I take action the discomfort of doing the task will be over quickly and perhaps more quickly than the discomfort I will face from having put off the task.'*

• Irrational Belief: *'Housework is boring and takes up lots of time. It shouldn't be necessary for me to do housework.'*
Challenge: *'Everyone has things they don't want to do. There is no rational reason why it shouldn't be*

necessary for me to do tasks I don't want to do. I have done things I don't want to do before and felt satisfaction with myself once they were completed.'

Some of the beliefs underlying procrastination may seem very plausible and rational. The way to test out how reasonable they really are in a particular situation is to think: 'If I don't do this now, will I regret it later?'

If you know that you may well have future regrets if you put off a task, it is better to take action now. Not taking action will trigger stress.

5. 'Must', 'should' and 'have to' beliefs
These beliefs are responsible for much of the faulty thinking behind stress.

Challenging stress induced by 'must', 'should' and 'have to' beliefs
Use your ABC sheets to identify and dispute these irrational beliefs, turning them into preferences. For example:

• Belief: '*I must not make a fool of myself when I speak at today's meeting.*'
Challenge: '*I would prefer not to make a fool of myself. However, if I do, I will still survive. I have survived worse. What would happen if I just gave it a go anyway?*'

Identify new, more useful beliefs and check out your new assumptions. For example, what would really happen if you raised a point at today's business meeting?

must know

Tricks to overcome stress linked to procrastination
• Challenge your inertia: set yourself a project or goal and spend at least five minutes a day on it.
• Give yourself a routine: set yourself specific times of day to do specific little tasks.
• Don't allow yourself to do things you usually do until you have done at least one thing you don't usually do.
• Learn new skills: if you lack organization or prioritization skills ask someone to teach you.
• Give yourself rewards: reward yourself with a treat of some kind for every small task you complete. For example, how about putting money into a treat box?
• Give yourself penalties: every time you put off a task, make sure you apply a pre-thought-out penalty (which will really cause you irritation!), e.g. not being able to watch a favourite TV programme.

Look on the bright side

A study in 2001 showed that people who had an optimistic view of the world had half the risk of coronary heart disease compared to more pessimistic people.

Extra stress busters

Put your difficulties in proportion

Do you know how other people feel? You may not be the only person who has these fears. Perhaps you can learn to share and thereby reduce difficulties.

Become active

Stressed people tend to be more passive in their attitude to life than optimistic people. Taking action and becoming more fully engaged and focused on what you are doing, taking responsibility for your actions and combating tendencies to procrastinate are all ways to destroy stress.

Exercise

Exercise and stress-busting are proven fellows. Exercise does not need to mean pain or strain. Any kind of activity or movement helps to improve the flow of blood and oxygen to the brain and lower stress and anxiety. If you don't normally do much exercise, even adding a 30-minute walk into your daily routine will help to combat stress.

Relaxation

The progressive relaxation method is given in Chapter 8. Here is an alternative relaxation and breathing method that you can try out.

Rhythmic breathing

1. **Sit with your back straight.** Keep your hands on the armrests or in your lap. Your eyes may be open or closed, whichever is most comfortable.
2. **Breathe in through your nose to the count of eight and out of your mouth to the count of eight.**

As you breathe in feel the breath filling up your lungs right down to the very bottom. With each breath you are taking in fresh oxygen. As you become practised in deep breathing, you will notice your breath filling up your stomach and then pushing your ribcage sideways so that it expands on the inward breath.

3. Hold the breath for four seconds then exhale for a count of eight. As you exhale, let the breath leave your body without effort, taking away any tensions and stresses. Gently relax your torso so all the breath is expelled. As the last of the breath is exhaled your stomach will naturally pull in. Hold your stomach in empty of air for four seconds. As you practise this breathing regularly, your stomach muscles will strengthen and you will feel more and more comfortable breathing for several minutes. With practice you can increase rhythmic breathing from five to ten minutes and up to half an hour or more. Breathe in groups of four inhales, holds and exhales. This stops you having any discomfort or hyperventilating.

want to know more?
• International Stress Management Association
www.isma.org.uk
• *Overcoming Traumatic Stress* by Claudia Herbert and Ann Wetmore, Constable and Robinson (1999)
• Chapter 2 explains the concept of faulty thinking.
• Read Chapter 11 to learn about the importance of self-esteem.

11 Self-esteem

This chapter helps you to understand what self-esteem really is and the faulty thinking that underlies a lack of it. You will learn here how to practise self-acceptance.

Self-esteem

Self-esteem is often referred to as a desirable goal, but what is it? According to the dictionary, if you esteem something you hold a good opinion of it, or give it worth or value.

must know

Self-esteem by any other name
Other words for self-esteem include:
- Self-image
- Self-opinion
- Self-confidence
- Self-respect
- Self-worth
- Self-perception
- Self-acceptance

What is self-esteem?

To have good self-esteem means that you have a good opinion of yourself – you judge your total self highly. Unwanted feelings are often founded on a low self-opinion – you either rate yourself low as a person or you evaluate your performance as a person poorly.

Low self-esteem

If you have a tendency to 'beat yourself up' or 'put yourself down' you may assume that you have to earn self-esteem or that you are only as good as your performance, which is measured against some 'ideal' benchmark. The trouble with using your achievements to earn a good self-opinion is that you may never reach this ideal and so may make yourself needlessly miserable.

At the heart of low self-esteem is a set of beliefs about yourself that form your identity and ideas about what you are capable of. These core beliefs will affect your thoughts and moods and what people and situations you attract to yourself.

Low self-esteem can develop sometimes if a child is told by a mother or father, 'You are bad' or 'You are good' when they have done something. This is poor use of language on the part of the parent. What they really mean is, 'You have behaved well' or 'You have behaved badly'. However, the child hears the words and takes them to mean 'I am a bad person and am unlovable or unworthy.'

High self-esteem

Conversely, an inaccurate and overinflated opinion of self-worth may also be harmful according to research. One study on thirteen-year-olds in six countries asked the teenagers to take a mathematics test and to rate their abilities before receiving their results. The American students rated most highly on self-esteem but came last in terms of actual results.

A study on violent offenders who had been involved in a variety of crimes from murder, rape and domestic violence to juvenile delinquency, found that these aggressive individuals scored highly on self-esteem – they rated themselves as superior to others.

It was concluded that people who have an over-inflated opinion of themselves may find it very difficult to recognize when they are engaging in over-risky or unhealthy behaviour.

The problems with self-rating and labelling

How do you strike a balance and find an accurate and rational assessment of self-worth? Your estimate of your own value and self-worth depends on the rating and labels you give yourself.

People with very low self-esteem rate or label themselves negatively. They use the type of faulty thinking referred to in Chapter 2 as 'labeling': I am a failure; I am useless; I am rubbish; I am bad; I am unlovable; I am not good enough; I am worthless; I am stupid.

must know

No labels
The real alternative to labelling yourself positively or negatively is not to rate or label yourself at all – instead practise accepting yourself.

must know

Self-acceptance
Self-acceptance allows
a balanced self-
perception which allows
you to be a complex
'warts and all' person

People with overinflated self-esteem rate or label themselves highly: I am the best; I am superhuman; I am talented and popular; I am better than other people.

The innate difficulty of rating or labelling in pursuit of self-esteem is that we have to perform complex calculations based on our performance. Our brains are unconsciously adding up the value of our performance in relationships, say, versus our lack of performance in our work. The only way the brain can cope is to keep everything as simple as possible by using black and white thinking and labelling. Instead of noticing what has gone well and what is going badly, it only notices what has gone badly and deletes the rest.

A self-rater/labeller thinks in this way: I am good at sports so I am a success; I once had a bad relationship so I am a failure. This then feeds a vicious circle of negativity about self and lower and lower self-esteem.

There is an alternative to rating yourself at one extreme or another. It is a thinking error to assume that the only alternative to a negative label is a positive one. This irrational black and white way of thinking assumes that you either have to be good or bad, you are a success or a failure. If you have low self-esteem you 'should' practise and build high self-esteem. The flaw in this is that if you set out to achieve high self-esteem you are still focusing on self-labelling and self-rating.

Self-acceptance
Self-acceptance means that instead of rating yourself as a total person against what you do, you

accept your behaviour and refrain from drawing conclusions about what it means about you as a person. Instead you have a more balanced perception of yourself that allows for the fact that you are a complex person with many facets – warts, diamonds and everything in between.

For example, imagine that your wife complains that you forgot to take the dry cleaning to the cleaners. With low self-esteem, the following thoughts might come into your mind: 'I'm a total failure; I can never do anything right; I am stupid!' These thoughts cause you to feel depressed and sad. You are labelling and rating yourself as a complete person based on your performance.

With self-acceptance, what you would do instead would be to get rid of the labels all together. You might think: 'when I don't pay attention to my to-do list, it has consequences for me I don't like; this is something I do often; what can I do to make sure I remember to pay attention to my to-do list?'

Notice that with self-acceptance, you don't draw a line between your behaviour and you as a person. If you fail at some performance target you have set yourself, you won't feel worse about yourself. You refrain from any negative labelling.

Now, what would happen instead if you were to say, 'I remembered to take the dry cleaning to the cleaners. I am a fantastic person.'? The danger here is that you are still drawing conclusions about yourself based on your performance and polarity or black and white thinking. The harm in this potentially is that the next time you forget to do something, you will slip back into a negative judgement about yourself – if high performance provides evidence that you are a

watch out

What happens when you don't accept yourself
• You look for others to make you complete.
• You hunt for love from others.
• You stop your own growth and learning through fear of what finding out the truth about yourself might reveal.
• You don't accept your past, present or future.
• You view parts of your life as wasted.
• You try to hide from yourself.
• You are sensitive to rejection.
• You beat yourself up at the first sign of underperformance.
• You compare yourself with others and try to beat them.
• You don't live in the present.
• You try to win self-esteem through achievements and material possessions.

must know

What happens when you accept yourself
• You allow yourself to grow.
• You accept other people as well.
• You replace judgement with love.
• You face the truth.
• You look forward to what you can learn about yourself every day in new situations.
• You look at the past, present and future as positive and meaningful.
• You forgive easily.

good, successful person, poor performance may still provide evidence for negative labelling and feeling sad or depressed.

How to stop self-labelling and self-rating and learn self-acceptance

As with all change, getting rid of self-rating and labelling takes practice, application and choice. You will know when you have changed when you can accept yourself as you are in all your parts, where you are right now. Repetition will build new habits and reinforce them over time until they become your new, automatic thought patterns, replacing old thinking errors.

True self-esteem is true self-acceptance – unconditionally accepting ourselves as we are. Self-acceptance is based around a set of beliefs about people that lead to different thinking choices.

1. **Human beings are complex.** You are more than one thing or another. You are not black or white. You have different aspects and degrees. As a result you can never rate or label yourself accurately or put yourself into a neat box. Self-acceptance involves accepting and forgiving yourself and others for being human.

2. **You are unique.** There is no one exactly like you. There is no one who thinks exactly like you. Stop making comparisons with other people. Acceptance is about enjoying who you are.

3. **People are always changing and developing over time.** Albert Ellis said, 'People's intrinsic value or worth cannot really be measured accurately because their being includes their becoming.'

4. **Human beings are fallible and imperfect.**

If we do amazingly well at something, it doesn't make us perfect. If we do very badly at something we still do some things right so we are not imperfect either. Throughout your life you will make mistakes so it is better to view them as useful feedback rather than an indication of an absolute failure. This belief stops us from blaming ourselves and others too much when something we don't want happens.

Once you have accepted yourself as you are, you can then focus on what you do, what your goals are and any changes you would like to make to what you do. With unconditional self-acceptance, this is not because you 'have to' or 'should' change anything to be an OK person but because you will feel good about what have done.

The Rosenberg Self-esteem Scale

The Rosenberg Self-esteem Scale (used here with permission) is one of the most widely used self-esteem measures in social science research. Developed by Dr M. Rosenberg, who was a professor of Sociology at the University of Maryland, it is based on studies in the 1960s of 5,024 high-school students.

On page 188 is a list of statements dealing with your general feelings about yourself. If you strongly agree with a statement, circle SA; if you agree, circle A; if you disagree, circle D; if you strongly disagree, circle SD.

The scale ranges from 0–30, with 30 indicating the highest score possible. Scores between 15 and 25 are within normal range; scores below 15 suggest low self-esteem.

must know

Self-acceptance exercise
Look at yourself in a mirror. Look straight into your own eyes and then look at your face as a whole. Look at all the bits of you that you do and don't like. Don't ignore anything. Take all aspects of yourself in. Say to yourself three times, 'No matter what my flaws are I accept myself totally and completely'. The more you do this the easier it will get.

11 Self-esteem

	1. Strongly Agree	2. Agree	3. Disagree	4. Strongly Disagree
1 I feel that I'm a person of worth, at least on an equal plane with others.	SA	A	D	SD
2 I feel that I have a number of good qualities.	SA	A	D	SD
3 All in all, I am inclined to feel that I am a failure.	SA	A	D	SD
4 I am able to do things as well as most other people.	SA	A	D	SD
5 I feel I do not have much to be proud of.	SA	A	D	SD
6 I take a positive attitude toward myself.	SA	A	D	SD
7 On the whole, I am satisfied with myself.	SA	A	D	SD
8 I wish I could have more respect for myself.	SA	A	D	SD
9 I certainly feel useless at times.	SA	A	D	SD
10 At times I think I am no good at all.	SA	A	D	SD

Rosenberg Scale: Rosenberg, Morris; 1989. *Society and the Adolescent Self-Image*, revised edition, Middletown, CT: Wesleyan University Press.

For items 1, 2, 4, 6 and 7

Strongly agree = 3

Agree = 2

Disagree = 1

Strongly disagree = 0

For items 3, 5, 8, 9 and 10

Strongly agree = 0

Agree = 1

Disagree = 2

Strongly disagree = 3

The simplest way to use this scale yourself is to take a copy of it and check your answers before and after a programme of CBT to see how positively your self-assessment has changed over time. There are no discrete cut-off points to delineate high and low self-esteem.

want to know more?
• *Overcoming Low Self-esteem* by Melanie Fennell, Constable and Robinson, 1999
• Chapter 2 explains the principles of faulty thinking.
• Chapter 10 has important advice on anger.

Useful organizations

- **Association for Cognitive Analytic Therapy** www.acat.me.uk
- **Association for Rational Emotive Behaviour Therapy** www.rebt.bizland.com
- **Association for Behavioural and Cognitive Therapies** www.abct.org
- **Beating the Blues:** www.ultrasis.com/products/product.jsp?product_id=1
- **The Beck Institute for cognitive therapy and research** www.beckinstitute.org
- **British Association for Behavioural and Cognitive Psychotherapies (BABCP)** The leading CBT body in the UK, it provides information on CBT and searches for accredited therapists. www.babcp.com
- **British Association for Counselling and Psychotherapy (BACP)** www.bacp.co.uk
- **The British Psychological Society** www.bps.org.uk
- **Calipso website:** www.calipso.co.uk
- **Depression Alliance** www.depressionalliance.org
- **European Association for Behaviour and Cognitive Therapies** www.eabct.com

- **First Steps to Freedom** www.first-steps.org (phobias, panic attacks, general anxiety and obsessive-compulsive disorders)
- **The International Association for Cognitive Psychotherapy** www.cognitivetherapyassociation.org
- **International Stress Management Association UK (ISMA)** www.isma.org.uk
- **National Institute for Health and Clinical Excellence**, www.nice.org.uk UK government sponsored organization giving reports and guidelines on various disorders and treatments
- **National Phobics' Society** www.phobics-society.org.uk
- **OCD Action** www.ocdaction.org.uk Help for obsessive-compulsive disorder (OCD) and other disorders such as body dysmorphic disorder (BDD)
- **Triumph Over Phobia (TOPUK)** www.triumphoverphobia.com
- **United Kingdom Council for Psychotherapy (UKCP)** www.psychotherapy.org.uk

Further reading

The Feeling Good Handbook, D. D. Burns, Penguin, 1990

Love is Never Enough, A. T. Beck, Penguin, 1988

Mind Over Mood: a cognitive therapy treatment manual for clients, D. Greenberger, C. A. Padesky, Guilford, 1995

The Anger Control Workbook: simple, innovative techniques for managing anger and developing healthier ways of relating, M. McKay, P. Rogers, New Harbinger Press, 2000

The Assertiveness Workbook: how to express your ideas and stand up for yourself at work and in relationships, R. J. Paterson, New Harbinger Press, 2000

Cognitive-Behavioral Therapy for Bipolar Disorder, Monica Ramirez Basco and A. John Rush, Guilford, 1996

Cognitive-Behavioural Counselling in Action (Counselling in Action series), Peter Trower, Andrew Casey, and Windy Dryden, Sage Publications, 1988

Cognitive Behaviour Therapy for Chronic Medical Problems, Craig A. White, John Wiley & Sons, 2001

Cognitive Therapy of Anxiety Disorders: A Practical Guide, Adrian Wells, John Wiley & Sons, 1997

The 'Overcoming' series of books: based on the concepts of CBT to help people combat problems:

- *Overcoming Anxiety*, H. Kennerley, Robinson, 1997
- *Overcoming Depression*, P. Gilbert, Robinson, 2000
- *Overcoming Low Self-esteem*, M. Fennell, Robinson, 1999
- *Overcoming Panic*, D. Silove, V. Manicavasagar, Robinson, 1997
- *Overcoming Social Anxiety and Shyness*, G. Butler, Robinson, 1999
- *Overcoming Childhood Trauma*, H. Kennerley, Robinson, 2000

Free online CBT resources

- **Mood Gym**: moodgym.anu.edu.au
  Australian-based CBT website for use with depression
- **Living Life to the Full:**
  www.livinglifetothefull.com
  Skills training for patients and carers

- **Fear Fighter:** www.fearfighter.com
  Your doctor can give you access to this website
- **Ultrasis:** www.ultrasis.com
  They produce interactive, computer-based CBT programmes

Index

agoraphobia 11, 144
anger 11, 17, 42, 44-7, 53, 113-31
assertiveness 119-24
defeating 116-19
faulty thinking behind anger 115
forgiveness 125-30
and health 114
negative effects 115
anxiety 10, 11, 19, 20, 23, 37, 46, 64, 74, 104, 108, 110, 133-47, 168
changing faulty self-talk 140-42
disorders 142-6
lifestyle changes 137
monitoring progress 146-7
overcoming 137-9
symptoms 134, 135
understanding 134-7

Beck, Aaron 12, 13
belief rating 99-100
breathing 178-9

caffeine 137
calmness 105, 108
Camera Check of Perception 92
change, objections to 108-11
Cognitive Behavioural Therapy
how it works 13
what it means 10
why use it? 10-11

depression 10, 11, 20-23, 37, 39, 74-5, 104, 108, 114, 135, 149-65
combating 155-65
development 151-3
rumination 153, 155
symptoms 150-51, 154
diaries 101, 145-6, 157, 160
drinking 22, 135, 137
drug-taking 22, 135

eating disorders 11
Ellis, Dr Albert 13, 14, 19, 20, 186
empathy 129
exercise 137, 178

facing problems 73
failure 107, 108
fears 10, 11, 49, 50, 60, 70, 136, 137
feeling checklist 98
foods 137
forgiveness 125-30
frustration 42, 53

guilt 11, 42, 45

happiness 71, 73, 74, 108
Holmes-Rahe Social Readjustment Scale 172-4

insomnia see sleep problems

jealousy 19, 39

Maslow, Abraham 48
Maslow's Hierarchy of Needs 46, 48
Maultsby, M.C. 13, 92
mood diary 101

negative reinforcement 12, 15
negative thinking 10, 15-18, 49, 68, 108, 161

obsessions 12, 143, 146
obsessive-compulsive disorder (OCD) 11, 145-6
organizations 190
overeating 22, 135

panic attacks 11, 47, 64, 133, 134, 136, 143
Pavlov, Ivan 11, 13
phobias 10, 11, 12, 143-5
positive reinforcement 12, 15, 68
post-traumatic stress disorder 11

Rational Emotive Therapy 14, 19
relationships 11, 21, 28, 31-2, 35, 37, 69, 88-9, 91-2, 94, 95, 120, 130, 164
relaxation 137-40, 178
resentment 42, 45, 46
responsibilities 122
rights 122

Rosenberg, Dr M. 187
Rosenberg Self-esteem Scale 187-9

schizophrenia 11
self-acceptance 125-6, 131, 181, 184-7
self-esteem 37, 52, 181-9
Rosenberg Self-esteem Scale 187-9
what it is 182-7
shame 105, 106
sleep problems 11, 39, 168
SMART goals 80-82
social phobia 11, 144-5
stress and tension 11, 20, 22, 64, 167-79
cause of stress 169
effects of stress 171
extra stress busters 178-9
modern life and stress 168-9
signs of stress 173
stress mismatch 169
stress potential 171-7
studying 36, 55
success 107-8
symptom stress 20

therapist, finding a 75
therapy sessions 23

weight problems 28, 29, 37, 51, 64, 81
worries 49-50, 60, 64, 134, 136